Granddaughters of the Holocaust

Never Forgetting What They Didn't Experience

Psychoanalysis and Jewish Life

The *Psychoanalysis and Jewish Life* book series has been established to promote scholarship, research, and a wide range of theoretical, textural, and clinical studies on the multiple interconnections between and mutual influence of Judaism and contemporary psychoanalysis. Its aim is broad, spanning a wide variety of subject areas: from the origins of psychoanalysis in Jewish circles in turn-of-the-century Vienna to clinical studies illuminating contemporary facets of Jewish identity and self-understanding; from explorations of psychological aspects of Jewish theology to psychoanalytic investigations of anti-Semitism; from studies of Jewish religious ritual to analyses of Hasidic mysticism and folklore; from psychoanalytic studies of pre-World War II Yiddish theater to the clinical practice of psychoanalysis in contemporary Israel. The *Psychoanalysis and Jewish Life* book series provides a home for fresh and intellectually challenging contributions across the spectrum of this interdisciplinary area of scholarship.

* * *

We are quickly approaching a time in which the survivors of the Shoah will no longer be with us to bear testimony to their experiences. As we approach this era, new studies have been undertaken not only of the second generation of the survivors' children, but now of the third generation, the survivors' grandchildren. The *Psychoanalysis and Jewish Life* Book Series is proud to publish *Granddaughters of the Holocaust: Never Forgetting What They Didn't Experience*, one of the first book-length studies of this kind. Nirit Gradwohl Pisano, herself the granddaughter of survivors, presents a qualitative study of in-depth interviews of Americans and Israelis who are part of this third generation. Dori Laub, one of the pioneers of qualitative research and psychoanalytic interviewing of survivors, contributes an introduction to this moving and insightful study, which will help facilitate further research and investigation of the intergenerational transmission of trauma and resilience.

—Lewis Aron

Series Editor: Lewis Aron, PhD, New York University, New York

Editorial Board:
Susannah Heschel, PhD, Dartmouth College, Hanover
Arnold Richards, MD New York University, New York
Jill Salberg, PhD New York University, New York
Moshe Halevi Spero, PhD, Bar-Ilan University, Ramat Gan
Karen Staff, PsyD, Long Island University at C.W. Post, Brookville, New York

GRANDDAUGHTERS OF THE HOLOCAUST

Never Forgetting What They Didn't Experience

NIRIT GRADWOHL PISANO

FOREWORD BY DORI LAUB

Boston 2013

Library of Congress Cataloging-in-Publication Data:
A catalog record for this title is available from the Library of Congress.

Copyright © 2012 Academic Studies Press
All rights reserved
ISBN 978-1-936235-88-9 (hardcover)
ISBN 978-1-618112-97-2 (paperback)

Book design and cover photo by Adell Medovoy

Published by Academic Studies Press in 2012, paperback edition 2013.
28 Montfern Avenue
Brighton, MA 02135, USA

press@academicstudiespress.com
www.academicstudiespress.com

אם אין אני לי, מי לי; וכשאני לעצמי, מה אני; ואם לא עכשיו, אימתי.
פרקי אבות, פרק א, משנה יד.

If I am not for myself, who will be for me?
If I am only for myself, what am I?
And if not now, when?
Ethics of the Fathers, 1: 14

ACKNOWLEDGMENTS

> Since then, at an uncertain hour,
> That agony returns,
> And till my ghastly tale is told
> This heart within me burns.
> —Samuel Taylor Coleridge, 1798, p. 208

The Drowned and the Saved, Primo Levi's final memoir, which was first published months after his suicide in April of 1987, opens with the above quote. Twenty-two years later, in April of 2009, I arrived in Jerusalem for my grandmother's funeral. The shock and sorrow of her passing had taken residence in my throat. In a hurried visit to her modern, new apartment overlooking the ancient city, I was struck first by the light, and then by my grandmother's tangible presence in this home that I had not yet visited. I deeply and consolingly inhaled the familiar: the "Shalom" tile on her wall, bearing the image of a dove clutching an olive branch, which is now awkwardly hanging in my New York City apartment; the leftover pita, hummus, and Emek cheese stacked neatly in her refrigerator, which we heartbreakingly discarded moments later in preparation for Passover; the collage of my late grandfather's photos assembled in the bedroom, alongside pictures of her children, grandchildren, and great-grandchildren scattered throughout the apartment. And then I saw it. The sole item on her nightstand, embracing the edge of her bed, it appeared both horribly out of place yet entirely appropriate: Primo Levi's *The Drowned and the Saved*, as though she had been reading such books all along. In her final days, it seems, my grandmother courageously found her way back to the beginning.

Sensing the conclusion of my research on the horizon, and anxiously fantasizing how the final work might be received by my family, the presence of Levi's book confirmed on that day what I had unconsciously known: that my grandmother has accompanied me on this journey from the start, exploring the inexplicable, inviting the obscene, determinedly evolving our shared history. I offer my grandmother my deepest gratitude, admiration, and love. This study is dedicated to her, a pillar of strength and support, and to all of the extraordinary people who continue to reflect on their histories – ensuring that the most painful memories and frightening conversations are integrated in our ongoing collective narratives.

I would like to express my immense gratitude to the women who sat down for an interview and opened up their world. Their narratives provide a glimpse into history and remind us to "Never forget."

My sincerest appreciation goes to Michael O'Loughlin, my mentor and confidant, who gave me permission to discover the "research" that resonates with who I am. I look forward to our ongoing exploration of truth, and collaboration in the quest of bearing witness. Many thanks also to my editor, Lewis Aron, who provided the refueling push I needed to integrate my evolution and realize my place within this work.

Finally, I offer my deepest gratitude to my loving and supportive family, who joined me in my challenging journey through the world of history and psychology, and inspired me to uncover my own voice.

TABLE OF CONTENTS

FOREWORD *by Dori Laub, MD* ... 11

PREFACE ... 16

CHAPTER 1: REVIEW OF THE LITERATURE ... 20
    The Broken Link ... 20
    Intergenerational Transmission of Trauma ... 24
    Jewish Americans and the Holocaust ... 29
    The Incorporation of the Holocaust in Israeli Identity ... 33
    Combat and Loss, Solidarity and Pride ... 37
    The Third Generation of the Holocaust ... 40

CHAPTER 2: RESEARCH APPROACH ... 47

CHAPTER 3: BETHANY ... 51
    Constructing a Narrative in Silence and Absence ... 52
    The Mechanism of Transmission ... 57

CHAPTER 4: LEAH ... 64
    Secrets... ... 65
    ... Ghosts... ... 68
    ... And Surrounding Shadows ... 74

CHAPTER 5: YAEL ... 77
    Past Becomes Present... ... 80
    ... And Present Becomes Past ... 86

CHAPTER 6: REBECCA ... 90
    Attempts at a "Rational" Life ... 90
    Day-to-Day Amidst the Irrational ... 94

CHAPTER 7: SAMANTHA ... 102
    Holocaust Trauma: One, Two, Three Generations ... 102
    First Glimpses into Generation Number Four ... 111

CHAPTER 8: RUTH ... 117
    Shame... or Pride ... 117
    But Ever-Present... Fear ... 121

CHAPTER 9: MIRIAM	128
Binging on History	132
Attempting to Restrict the Past	134
Maintaining Weight and Substance	137
CHAPTER 10: MALKA	140
"There's Simply No One"	142
"Such a Big Deal"	146
CHAPTER 11: JESSICA	154
Without Memory or Desire	154
Reconstructing Memory	160
CHAPTER 12: BRIANA	165
It's Not You, It's Me	165
It's Not Me, It's You	171
CHAPTER 13: DISCUSSION	176
Reworking Trauma Trails: Possibilities for Resilience	176
EPILOGUE	183
Life Before This Study	183
Fully Inside It	185
Coming Out of the Experience, Or Not	188
REFERENCES	191
INDEX	198

FOREWORD

Dori Laub, MD

The greatest merit of this book is that it illuminates an arena we suspected existed, that we anecdotally described, and that we perhaps even published individual case studies about: the effects of the Holocaust on the third generation. An extensive body of literature exists on the second generation—they were the first absorbers of the shock—and clinicians have been looking with expectancy and fear for the effect on the third generation. In an era of globalization, of revolutionary changes in communication, and of an ever growing tendency to level differences and standardize life, do historical experiences still play a central role in one's psychological makeup?

The book, as it is written, is a passionate journey in the search for a truthful answer to this question. It examines the same history played out in a variety of plots, and it is this very variety which upholds the conclusion that such an effect is very much present and tangible. The book is not about a sweeping foreclosing generalization; it is rather about a tedious struggle for knowing, against traumatic erasure and mutedness.

The methodology used—interpretative research of psychoanalytic interviews of ten granddaughters of survivors of the Holocaust and the concurrent reflections of the interviewer—allows for the creation of ten case studies in which three-dimensional, full-bodied, colorful, and nuanced characters emerge, who have a personality, a life, and a family history framed by very specific patterns of conflict and defense. This is by far more informative and enriching than the abstract themes that emerge in the studies utilizing content analysis or would-be quantitative analysis of traits that have until now been performed in this population. The ten granddaughters feel present in the room while one reads about them. They are not clichés. What is further stunning is the wealth of data that emerges from an interview of an hour and a half and a close recording of the interviewer's own reflections, associations, and countertransference observations. It is as if the course of a whole treatment has been captured in that one interview. Most likely it is the urge to give testimony, "the testimonial momentum," and the presence of a totally attuned listener that together drive the process to reach such extraordinary results.

All ten granddaughters acknowledge the powerful omnipresence of the historical trauma of the Holocaust in their current lives. The degree to which each one of them takes possession of it and makes a conscious decision regarding how to contain and address it varies. Some are fully aware of it and able to make life choices that are outside its impact; others are aware of it but cannot help letting it dictate various positions they take in life; still others, while powerfully aware of its emotional impact, cannot clearly define it, nor tease out the role it plays in their life. In the latter group, a vague fear that they are helpless to shape their lives and will inevitably succumb, so that future generations will continue to be affected, prevails.

It bears repeating that all of the ten granddaughters acknowledge the presence of the traumatic history of the Holocaust in their lives. It is this universe of undigested, unassimilated experiences, shards of a broken world, which ties them together. The word "camp" is perhaps the best that can be used to illustrate this tie. While for everyone else its connotation is to a summer camp, for them it reverberates with what their parents and grandparents have or have not told them about their WWII experiences.

This preface will highlight two topics: a) how the granddaughters differ in their experience of the Holocaust, and b) how they variably respond to these experiences. The Holocaust has transformed the everyday experiences of most of these individuals into events with traumatically layered meaning.

Bethany is struck by how little is verbally acknowledged. This phenomenon is discussed as "a shelter of silence that has become a Holocaust memorial." She speaks to the idea that "it is as though the Holocaust is being relived in silence." She has to call her father during the interview and apologizes profusely because he thought she had died when his call to come and pick her up was delayed. For Bethany, nothing else existed so long as Holocaust traumas did.

Yael feels almost cheated at having been born after the Holocaust and not having experienced it directly. Not knowing each other's whereabouts is very frightening to Yael, her mother, and her grandmother, resonating so much with the Nazi times, when people would just disappear.

Leah grew up with a paternal great aunt who kept dozens of suitcases packed, ready for an unexpected move, and with the ever-present image of a five-year-old son shot by the Nazis in the street, in front of her maternal grandmother.

Samantha and Jessica grew up with a grandfather, an Auschwitz survivor, who suffered from scleroderma and from a physically abusive bipolar wife who would hit him with a menorah. He tried to speak but could barely whisper. The murmurs of his memory were met with a refusal. His daughter, being the only caretaker of her suicidal parents, directed her rage at her children. While Jessica dissociated and suffers from explicitly non-Holocaust related nightmares that someone is trying to kill her, Samantha retained her clarity as to how the first and second generation reenacted the trauma, leaving the third generation dazzled and terrified. She is constantly on alert and anxious not to repeat it.

Miriam tried to establish boundaries by rebelling, binging and purging, and refraining from watching or reading Holocaust movies or books. Malka recognizes how events that occur in the present take the meanings of things that happened in the past, and that she is forever paying back something she does not owe. Briana, whose paternal grandparents are Holocaust survivors who felt very guilty for surviving—not good enough to deserve it—was always crying about it. Her grandparents' guilt was passed on to her father, who was never praised, and to Briana, who felt she had no right to feel pain because others suffered more. She has frightening dreams about the Holocaust—including feelings of terror at being found, at being buried alive, of Nazis all around, etc.

In response, each of them dealt with the intergenerationally transmitted Holocaust trauma very differently. In Briana's case, there were years of anorexia in response to her father's transgenerationally transmitted judgment of not being good enough, not deserving his survival. Her father wanted to make her eat, not talk about it. Leah's obsessive-compulsive rituals and routines were a way of putting order back into "something massive having gone off course"—the ghostly face of the 5-year-old boy who had been shot in front of his mother, appearing in every face of the family, and perhaps even in every human face. Yael's idealization of a heroic grandfather, who grasped that he had to place himself in the front of the wheelbarrow carrying the dead corpses from the gas chambers to the crematoria in order to not be shot, eclipsed everything else in her life. With his death, everything was lost. She suffers from a recurring nightmare of being chased by an army of Red Coats. Miriam, who chose a Slovak (whom she found extremely exciting) to be her first love, did so as a rebellion against both her grandmother's trying to forget her sadness and her mother's trying to recover and contain it.

Samantha struggles with food-related conflicts and panic attacks and Jessica lives in a hazy, elusive world. They are sisters, granddaughters of the above-mentioned severely abused and suicidal Auschwitz survivor. Their mother, his daughter, vacillated between excessive secrecy and excessive disclosure, particularly with Samantha. Their mother was exhausted and enraged at being the sole caretaker of her parents, and took it out on her children. While Samantha recognizes her own inability to fully bear witness to the overpowering nature of her experiences, she still feels that "everything could just end" and does all she can to avoid reenactments of "losing her cool." Her sister Jessica dissociates, feels she must have done something wrong to cause such fury in her mother, and cries all the time—especially in her therapy. A sense of helplessness prevails, knowing that she carries in her three generations of unexpressed feelings.

The larger the communicative gap, the more determined the refusal to listen; the more violent the clash, the more unbridgeable the divide. Although Rebecca kept asserting that "she is fine with it"—the interviewer felt she was treading lightly in the interview. Her senile grandfather called her mother a Nazi for proposing to transfer him from his current home to an assisted living situation. In return, he is described as being insane—a label that does not explore his experience of being relocated, institutionalized once again in his life. Growing up, his children refused to listen to stories, and the two generations lived in two separate worlds. Rebecca's flight is a flight into rationality. In an entirely different manner, Ruth, who also refused to hear her grandfather's stories, of how his baby sister Toni, age 12, was killed right away, is plagued by shame for not having spoken up when she saw a swastika in Madrid, Spain, and decides that it is her responsibility to carry on being a Jew and be proud of it. She has a strong sense of "history unfolding in the present."

Many of the granddaughters feel it is their function to continue or even to complete the "feeling work" that remains to be done to unlock the intergenerational trauma—to make conscious the "unthought known." They realize that "it is precisely in not knowing, in the utter lack of history, that trauma is transmitted". Their challenge is heightened by the denial and dissociation of the two preceding generations.

Bethany has become the "narrator" of the family who serves her grandparents and her father as a bridge back to life. She has dedicated herself to curing her ancestors' trauma, and she wants to live a life that will undo this history. Malka feels it is the women who are the carriers of the stories, handing them down from generation to generation. Her history is her "baby" and she is doing everything to keep it alive. She is the one who recognizes (and translates) how events that occur in the present take the meaning of things that happened in the past. Her father, even now, is coming in running in the middle of the night, to see if she is still there. Briana is the overly expressive member in the family who carries the emotions of various generations.

I have briefly reviewed the individualized unique experience of the Holocaust in each of the ten granddaughters and the equally unique response each one of them had to that experience. It goes without saying that history is very much alive and ongoing, and takes on a very personalized meaning in each one of them. One must read the book in its entirety in order to appreciate that.

Having taken testimonies of survivors myself, I can appreciate the hard work it took to carry out these interviews and, even more than that, to write them up and put them together. The level of self discipline required is simply exemplary. Repeatedly one has to pull back and avoid the pitfalls of a simplifying generalization and a premature foreclosure based on rushed and incomplete "understanding"; the latter comes to be a hugely powerful temptation when one attempts to unravel the convoluted and intertwined residual strains that remain in the wake of extreme traumatization.

PREFACE

As an Israeli-born, American-raised member of the third generation of the Holocaust, my identity is based on a mixture of Jewish and Israeli history, an amalgamation of past suffering and loss on the one hand, and emigration, hope, and renewal on the other. My paternal grandmother escaped Nazi Germany in 1938, at the age of seven, through the Kindertransport[1] to London. Aside from one sister, the remainder of her family perished in Auschwitz. Presumably, the younger girls were "lucky." The family members' parting on the train platform marked their eternal separation, and would continue to reverberate in my family's "goodbyes" for generations to come. At 16, my grandmother left her orphanage in London to make *aliyah*[2] and met my paternal grandfather, who would become the only rabbi in Bern, Switzerland, during the 1960s and 1970s. On my maternal side, my grandfather was born and raised in Amsterdam, and spent elementary school in a class with Anne Frank. He escaped to Switzerland via his father's Swiss passport in 1940, leaving his classmates behind. Throughout my life, I have recognized the value of my own Swiss passport, as it continues to provide a sense of relief, a kind of European "get out of jail card," (or get out of camp card), for my family and me.

My immediate family's relocation to the United States when I was seven years old was a world away from, yet highly reminiscent of, my grandmother's relocations at the same age two generations prior. In our life abroad, we cherished a sense of pride and resiliency, vehemently repeating the well-established Jewish motto, "Never again…" The intimately related but seemingly contradictory feelings of fear, guilt, and shame were left unacknowledged. We held three passports, spoke three languages, and successfully escaped the chaotic atmosphere of Israel, and more generally, of our past. While I had been taught a great deal

---

1   This is the rescue movement that took place in the months leading up to the outbreak of World War II. The United Kingdom took in approximately 10,000 Jewish children from Nazi Germany and the occupied territories.
2   The Hebrew word used to refer to Jewish immigration to Israel; literally "moving up." This is also the word used when a person is invited to recite a blessing over the Torah.

about the Holocaust, through stories, museums, books, and a personal trip to Auschwitz during high school, the sudden distance from my birthplace and its collective narrative further quieted the already faint memory of our traumatic history. I believe this distance provided me with an enhanced desire to seek out this topic and explore the manifestations of traumatic memory in the third generation. Along the way, I have discovered the ways in which my work serves as a testimony for my ancestors' experience.

My grandmother spent a lifetime shielding herself from the failure of language to depict her experience, and others from sharing her anguish. Understanding that some things must remain unsaid, her family attempted to "protect" their beloved wife and mother from her history. Of course, silence only further communicated her unimaginable suffering. Three generations following the event, as I sit with my interviewees, I invite them to share their historical curiosity, or lack thereof. "What are some of the questions you have always wanted to ask your grandparents?" I inquire. The questions imprinted in my mind, which I never successfully verbalized, include: What was it like to stand on a train platform at age seven, and wave goodbye to your family? How did you continue to exist following this separation? What happens now when you travel by train, interact with a seven-year-old, or say goodbye to a friend? I realize that what I am truly in search of are the forbidden feelings, the unspeakable and unfathomable emotions, which have been denied and transmitted in silence. While I never asked my grandmother these questions, and no longer have the opportunity to ask them, I am certain they will continue to shape who I am: "overly-sensitive," holding three generations' worth of unspoken emotions.

A number of issues arise from my brief familial account that I will address in this work, with the ultimate hope of better understanding the multifaceted and complex nature of identity formation vis-à-vis the intimate relationship between personal anecdote and collective memory. Of specific interest are the failures of language in communicating traumatic memory; the silence, myths, and taboos surrounding the Holocaust, during and after the birth of the State of Israel; and the unspoken but incessant transmission of traumatic memory following such catastrophe and humiliation. As can be seen in my own account, it is difficult to distinguish the origins of resiliencies from those of vulnerabilities, individual coping mechanisms from family and societal systems, or passion and pride from the intimately related experiences of fear, guilt, and shame. My individual story, merely one woman's narrative, simultaneously speaks to the struggle of a family, the development of a mentality, and the circumstances that impacted an entire civilization.

Contemporary Jews live in a world where the immediate memory of the Holocaust has faded, but culturally and psychologically transmitted residues of the Holocaust continue to manifest themselves. That is, while subsequent generations did not endure the horrors of the Holocaust directly, they did quite powerfully "absorb" the experiences, as stories pass from generation to generation, and communication transcends both verbal and nonverbal form. Unfathomable events are inevitably transmitted to and contained by the children and grandchildren of survivors.

The present work hones in on the intergenerational transmission of Holocaust trauma to the granddaughters of survivors. This group exposes the transmission pattern of Holocaust memories in a generation twice removed from the event itself, allowing for an additional perspective on family dynamics often unachieved by the children of survivors. The interviews conducted with these women offered an unencumbered space within which participants were asked to speak freely about their inheritance of Holocaust trauma and memory, and their responses to this legacy. Through words, behaviors, omissions, negations, and evasions, the resulting ten narratives provide startling evidence for the embodiment of ghostly echoes in the ways these women approach daily tasks of living and being. Thus, although the granddaughters of survivors did not themselves survive the Holocaust, they will, in a sense, "never forget what they didn't experience."

Unfortunately, silence surrounding historically traumatic events has the power to debilitate individuals and entire societies. Once a pattern of silence is established, shifting its contagious grip is a difficult undertaking, one that can span the realm of multiple generations. The act of narrating one's story—struggling to integrate thoughts and emotions in a coherent structure which feels accurate and acceptable to the narrator—is crucial for resilience to evolve. The nature of the narrative is secondary in importance: whether the narrator suppresses knowledge that exists beneath a thinly veiled surface, regurgitates a previously constructed account, or challenges herself in such a way that new narrative possibilities emerge, some type of story inevitably and remarkably unfolds. And, as content is disclosed and a process is revealed, even the unspeakable has a way of making its presence known. It is within this realm of language and beyond that the granddaughters of survivors can achieve a multi-generational perspective of their identities and bear witness as to what happened to their ancestors.

CHAPTER 1: REVIEW OF THE LITERATURE

> Within reach, close and not lost, there remained, in the midst of the losses, this one thing: language. This, the language, was not lost but remained, yet in spite of everything. But it had to pass through its own answerlessness, pass through a frightful falling mute, pass through the thousand darknesses of death bringing speech. It passed through and yielded no words for what was happening—but it went through those happenings. Went through, and could come into the light of day again, "enriched" by all that.
>
> —Paul Celan, 1958, p. 395

The Broken Link

Claude Lanzmann (1985), maker of the documentary *Shoah,* argued that any attempt to understand *Shoah*[1] is obscene. Nevertheless, as his film illustrates, engagement with the Holocaust and its legacy is essential. As Elie Wiesel noted, many survivors drew their will to survive from their belief in the importance of keeping memory of the exterminations alive. Attempts at narrating Holocaust memory can be found in works such as Wiesel's *Night* (1961), Spiegelman's *Maus* (1986, 1991), the writings of Améry, Borowski, and Levi, and in Lanzmann's *Shoah* (1985). These and the videotape archive collected by Dori Laub at Yale, and commentaries on that testimony (e.g., Langer, 1991), as well as the representational work being done at Holocaust museums worldwide, are attempts to symbolize an inexplicable event. As Holocaust archivist Dori Laub (1992) noted, *Shoah* is "An Event Without a Witness," in that anybody with a genuine understanding of the Holocaust was killed, and in that the Holocaust is incomprehensible and impossible to convey in words.

This sentiment is expanded in Davoine and Gaudillière's fundamental book, *History Beyond Trauma: Whereof One Cannot Speak, Thereof One*

1　The Hebrew word meaning "catastrophe," signifying the Holocaust.

Cannot Stay Silent (2004). The authors shed light on the complex nature of traumatic memories via a conceptualization of that which cannot be symbolized, an experience "outside the field of speech and beyond the mirror" (Davoine & Gaudillière, 2004, p. 45). As they explain, when a "catastrophe" falls beyond the scope of language—and words fail to even approach the horrific truths of history—distortions of memory are inevitable:

> The imminent catastrophe, the announced doomsday, has already happened but could not be inscribed in the past as past, since in this respect the subject of speech was not there. Nothing in the other was given him, no speech to name what happened there. Totally cut off, ignored, but also well known to everyone, sometimes uttered in history books and even advocated by the duty to remember though that made no difference, the truth was unable to be transmitted. The information has remained a dead letter, outside the field of speech (Davoine & Gaudillière, 2004, p. 29).

Within this framework, individuals suffering from psychosis are understood as desperately but often ineffectually attempting to merge the traumas of their personal histories with the traumas of history at large: because they do not possess the words for their experience, their existence unfolds outside of language. They cannot symbolize "what happened there," nor understand how "there" has overwhelmed the present, "here." Thus, in the absence of speech, their experiences have not been rightfully inscribed into the unconscious and then repressed; instead, they maintain the quality of being "erased, reduced to nothing, and yet inevitably existing" (Davoine & Gaudillière, 2004, p. 47). Along similar lines, survivors continue to live on condition that they repress or "cut out" their experiences and never look back, identified by Davoine and Gaudillière as "the cut out unconscious" (2004, p. 47). In order to achieve contact with this "cut out unconscious," there must be a willingness to engage in a new sort of "language game," a "silent language" in which one's story is shown, not spoken (Davoine & Gaudillière, 2004, p. 78-79). Yet, how can non-symbolic, nonverbal information be effectively communicated?

This conceptualization exposes the struggle of Holocaust survivors in a post-Holocaust world and challenges the relevance of survivors' *telling* of their tales. Langer's work, *Holocaust Testimonies: The Ruins of Memory* (1991), reveals the difficulty of conveying horrendous memories of the Holocaust in a contemporary world. A duality arises for survivors: on the one hand lies the "deep," "anguished," "humiliated," "tainted," and "unheroic" memory, and on the other hand, the "common" memory that clings to a benign sense of self and the world (Langer, 1991). Throughout their narratives and life experiences, survivors constantly shift back and forth between these two clashing existences: that of the traumatized self and that of the conventional self. While the latter position intermittently "restores the self" (Langer, 1991, p. 6), this constructive attitude is repeatedly disrupted by the haunting memories of devastating and unintegrated past events.

The sense of fragmentation therefore extends well beyond the act of telling a story for the sake of informing others, and is characteristic of survivors' attempts to exist in a post-Holocaust world. As one victim wonders, "After that, what are you supposed to do? You know what I'm saying? You're not supposed to see this; it doesn't go with life. These people come back, and you realize, they're all broken, they're all broken. Broken. Broken" (Langer, 1991, p. 136). The wounded identity and the shattered sense of agency further feed into this conflicted self:

> Witnesses remain divided between the knowledge that during their ordeal they were deprived of moral agency by their circumstances and their present need to see themselves then and now as the responsible agents of their own destiny and of those around them (Langer, 1991, p. 185).

Quite sensibly, then, Spiegelman's *Maus I and II* (1986, 1991) are founded on the idea that engagement with the Holocaust requires fictionalization: only the most absurd, nonsensical representations can symbolize the realities of this atrocity (Reilly, 1986).

Tarantelli (2003) writes of "a complete surrender to the process of disarticulation" during massive trauma, which "extinguishes even the most basic level of mental activity, contact with sensation, producing psychic and then psychogenic death" (p. 915). Tarantelli (2003) employs the metaphor of an "explosion" to capture the instantaneous psychological reaction to an external disaster (p. 916). Once something is completely destroyed and no existence is left, there is an "utter absence," an inability to observe that something because nothing remains to serve that purpose (Tarantelli, 2003, p. 916). This deadening void—in Grotstein's (1990b) terms "primary meaninglessness"—eliminates all other experience, such that the potential for meaning does not occur and the ability to register stimuli is impossible (Tarantelli, 2003). According to Matte Blanco (1988), "when we face emotions ... of an intensity which is felt as tending towards the infinite ... the experience of emotion leads one to feel the possibility of catastrophe, of disintegration" (p. 140; quoted by Tarantelli, 2003, p. 919). Thus, "psychogenic death" indicates a disruption of psychic energy and activity, wiping out consciousness, continuity, and any integration of self.

The process of disarticulation is unavoidable during massive psychic trauma, and the explosion eliminates a mind that might have endured the experience (Tarantelli, 2003). Even contact with physical sensation, which engages the mind's most primitive faculties, is entirely suspended under these circumstances. The explosion is all-pervading, such that the experience cannot be registered consciously by something outside of it because there *is* nothing outside of it (Tarantelli, 2003). In other words, the external and internal become one and the same. There is no "I-ness" (Ogden, 2001, p. 156; Tarantelli, 2003) that is separate from existence on the verge of extinction.

For a survivor of individual or collective trauma, experience unfolds outside of language, resisting symbolization. In her book, *The Unsayable: The Hidden Language of Trauma*, Rogers (2006) writes:

> What is so terrible about trauma is not abuse itself, no matter the brutality of treatment, but the way terror marks the body and then becomes invisible and inarticulate. This was the case even when someone could tell a story or reconstruct a memory. There was always something unsayable, too (p. 44).

Rogers (2006) beautifully portrays her work with victims of sexual abuse, illustrating her attempts to engage the silent communication of girls who were unwilling and unable to articulate their suffering.

Furthermore, she highlights the unspoken, unspeakable "language" of trauma, often observed through symptoms that manifest themselves on the body—symptoms which contemporary, categorical diagnoses fail to fully comprehend (Rogers, 2006).

The sayable versus "unsayable" is at the root of Lacanian views on language, in that language maintains the power to influence our "thoughts, demands, and desires" (Fink, 1999, p. 86). Lacan emphasizes the concept of "alienation" in language: "We have the sense, at times, that we cannot find the words to say what we mean, and that the words available to us miss the point, saying too much or too little. Yet without those words, the very realm of meaning would not exist for us at all" (Fink, 1999, p. 86). Because words are used as symbols within the realm of speech, a gap inevitably exists between the experience of a word and the actual thing it corresponds to. While for the neurotic patient language has been at least partly "subjectified," the psychotic patient constantly feels that he is "possessed" by language from the outside, as the symbols have not been truly absorbed (Fink, 1999, p. 87). This experience is familiar to the survivor of trauma. As explained by Davoine and Gaudillière, meaning depends on being able to find a place within language, successfully forming connections between thoughts and maintaining a social link with one's past (2004).

Boulanger (2005) highlights the "state of mindlessness" that characterizes the wounded self during massive psychic trauma: thoughts and reality become indistinguishable, such that connections between thoughts can lead to "terrifying meanings and untenable anxiety" (p. 23). Referencing Bion, Ogden, and Tarantelli, Boulanger reminds us of the value of "destroying links" during trauma, as dissociation can be self-protective during a time of overwhelming affects (2005, p. 23). Once broken, however, words lose their significance and the "unreflective world" takes over (Boulanger, 2005, p. 24). Alongside this break in contemplation and self-reflection, the mind loses its capacity to serve as a witness of events, a relater of testimony, and a bearer of meaning—for oneself, and, eventually, for future generations.

Intergenerational Transmission of Trauma

According to Davoine and Gaudillière (2004), a child easily and "paradoxically" becomes "the subject of the other's suffering, especially when this other is unable to feel anything" (p. 49). Through projective identification, the child thereby unexpectedly and unwillingly reenacts such a "hell" (Davoine & Gaudillière, 2004, p. 50). How does a child undertake her parents' suffering? In what way is trauma transmitted intergenerationally across families and entire communities? Can future generations heal the pain of a past they did not personally endure? Fraiberg, Adelson, and Shapiro's (1975) *Ghosts in the Nursery* examines these questions within a familial context, where members are "possessed by their ghosts ... while no one has issued an invitation, the ghosts take up residence and conduct the rehearsal of the family tragedy from a tattered script" (p. 165). The unspeakable past traumas experienced by the parents of Fraiberg et al's (1975) case studies were left unnamed and unprocessed, such that their mourning was foreclosed. The unmourned suffering silently escalated in power and magnitude, seizing lead roles in their lives and those of their children. Previous unresolved losses were thus transmitted to future generations.

What exactly happens with this powerful unmourned suffering? If the parent cannot recall it and will not speak of it, how does the child *know* its existence? In 1972, Judith Kestenberg initiated use of the term "transposition" to explain the psychological process of intergenerational transmission of massive trauma that occurs unconsciously (Kaplan, 1996). Transposition captures the phenomenon by which a parent's past experiences impinge upon the child's present being. Transposition has two distinct characteristics: first, it speaks to the immense "amount of psychological space" that the parent's history demands, and second, it refers to "reversals of ordinary time" between parent and child that leaves them in opposite chronological positions, with the child exceedingly an element of the parent's past (Kaplan, 1996, p. 224). Thus, the parent's history takes over the child's daily existence, forcing the child to abandon her right to live as an individual. Referencing a poem by Celan (1958), Kaplan writes: "the child suckles 'the black milk' of trauma, relishes and absorbs it, cultivates its bitter taste as if it were vital sustenance—as if it were existence itself" (1996, p. 224). Similarly, as Davoine and Gaudillière explain,

> Many small children have not received the words that would have allowed them to keep at bay the disasters experienced by their parents and ancestors. Rather, like

the children of Oedipus or Medea, they were abandoned, sacrificed on the battlefront of hatred, wars, and civil wars; they were armed with rifles, real or psychic, to be sent as human shields to protect the adults who remain in the rear (2004, p. 75).

That is, the child absorbs her parent's unmourned trauma as her own, devoting a lifetime to working through the internal devastation of their shared past. Because a transposition can arise at any given moment, the survivor parent's Holocaust history looms over the child's daily lifestyle:

> Though the mother still cannot remember her starvation, she transmits the emotional experience of starvation through her preoccupation with buying, preparing, serving, and eating food. The father transmits the physical degradations he endured by being preoccupied with cleanliness and the elimination of feces (Kaplan, 1996, p. 226).

At times, specifics such as a child's age may serve to trigger the re-enactment of history in present time; for example, Kaplan (1996) describes a hypothetical scenario of a girl who is "innocently competing with her mother for her father's attention" (p. 226), but happens to do so at the exact age that her mother was when she arrived in the Nazi camps. In Kaplan's example, the mother impulsively reacts by cutting off her daughter's ponytail, as this was done to her by Nazi soldiers. In response to this injury,

> The daughter develops an unconscious fantasy that she has been selected by her mother to perform a special mission. She, and she alone, can repair her mother's trauma by sacrificing her own desires and longings. She becomes obese, thus effectively concealing her beauty under layers of fat. Or she starves herself until her body is transformed into the body of a concentration camp survivor (Kaplan, 1996, p. 226-227).

A survivor parent who has lost family members in the Holocaust consciously wishes that her new, post-Holocaust family will replace the family members that were killed; the parent's unconscious wish, however, is that each new child or spouse will serve to reinstate the deceased (Kaplan, 1996, p. 234). For the child of a survivor, "the memorialization of the dead entails his resurrection ... The revenant knows she must fall into the interrupted biography of the dead one and complete it before she can carry on with her own life" (Kaplan, 1996, p. 234). In *Maus I and II*, Art Spiegelman (1986, 1991) skillfully captures the memorialization of the dead in telling the personal tale of his upbringing by a Holocaust survivor. Art, the post-Holocaust son, acts as a surrogate for his father's late son, Richieu, to such an extent that Art reports feeling throughout his life that he was in competition with a ghost. Indeed, in the final scene, his father calls Art "Richieu." Similarly, Vladek's new wife, Mala, endlessly falls short of reinstating his late wife, Anja. The enactments are rampant throughout both books: Art mutters that Vladek is a "murderer" for having destroyed his dead first wife's, Anja's, wartime diaries; Vladek yells at Art for making a mess with cigarette ash while talking about his experience of being yelled at by SS officers for making a mess in the camps; finally, Art's distance from Vladek sustains in him a sense of guilt for "mistreating" his father (Spiegelman, 1986, 1991).

Beyond all other vehicles, tormented silences serve as the main channel through which parents' unimaginable suffering can be witnessed by their children. Kaplan (1996) captures this immense authority of silence: "At first the child knows only that one or both parents are hiding some terrible secret. And the child wonders, 'What is the meaning of the absence, the silence? What is the truth that must never be spoken?'" (p. 219). Within this context, a survivor's child lives a "double life," in that present experiences bear the undercurrents of past events (p. 231). Everyday situations and mundane occurrences become instantaneously linked to both past and present:

> A loop of cord hanging from a lamp becomes a hangman's noose to the survivor. The child hears the parent gasp and sees the parent frantically rearranging the cord. A policeman approaches on the street; the mother has a panic attack. She clutches the child's hand tightly and stands as still as a statue. Nothing is said, but the child registers the mother's reactions and knows "something"

is wrong. The child comes to know that existence is precarious (Kaplan, 1996, p. 231).

Kaplan (1996) suggests that a child who senses her parent's terror, guilt, and shame" about something unfathomable is compelled to recreate such scenarios in order to concretize and ultimately cure the parent's trauma (p. 232). In a sense, Kaplan (1996) believes that it is only the survivor's children who can bear witness to their parent's history. Furthermore, a parent's secrecy can, in effect, drive the child's impulse to piece together what happened to the parent. "The parent unwittingly and against her conscious will positions her trauma within the child; the child sets out to cure the parent and undo her trauma by placing himself in the parent's position" (Kaplan, 1996, p. 224). Thus, it is the child's role to cure the parent's suffering through a number of contradictory tasks: "On the one hand, she is fighting to reinstate visions of love and goodness. On the other hand she represents the concretization of hatred" (Kaplan, 1996, p. 234-235). As a result, "She is expected to carry out and perform for her parent the unfinished work of mourning. Yet she is also expected to avenge the parents for the crimes committed against them by enacting the silenced hatred and rage" (Kaplan, 1996, p. 235).

Clearly, such duties take a toll on the child. At best, the child does not receive the necessary help in integrating her own experiences. At worst, deficits in a parent's empathic attunement to the child result in the child's experiences of overwhelming affect, impaired symbolization of experience, and a complete lack of meaningful integration of her feelings (Charles, 2003). Insufficient emotional development is passed along the generations, as affect remains a foreign and threatening experience. Furthermore, repeated exposure to shameful affects may lead to suppression or denial of those experiences through external tools such as compulsive eating and substance abuse (Charles, 2003). For these reasons, traumatic memories and familial reactions to history may only come to light over the course of several generations (Auerhahn & Laub, 1998, p. 22). "The barrage of experiences that patently ignore the child's perceived needs or feelings generates a sense of helplessness and meaninglessness before the hands of a cold and unseeing destiny, as the child who is not loved loses himself"—thus, the cycle is repeated (Charles, 2003, p. 72). Finally, because children's self-concepts are shaped by the circumstances of their upbringing, Charles (2003) argues that enactments reveal one's "helplessness in the face of destiny" (p. 73).

Auerhahn and Laub (1998) discuss ten forms of knowing massive psychic trauma, organized along a continuum that reflects the degree of psychological distance from, integration of, and ownership over the traumatic experience. These range from "not knowing"; to the replacement of disturbing memories with factual but less traumatizing ones; to states in which events are reenacted in an "altered state of consciousness"; to "compartmentalized, undigested fragments" of experience with "no conscious meaning or relation to oneself"; to "transference phenomena"; to a partial manifestation of the trauma in one's narrative; to its appearance in "compelling, identity-defining, and pervasive life themes"; to the integration of the trauma as a "witnessed narrative"; to its development as a "metaphor"; and to "action knowledge," where experience becomes consciously significant in such a way that it influences future decisions (Auerhahn & Laub, 1998, p. 23). Auerhahn and Laub maintain that survivors know mostly through fragments or transference phenomena, that children of survivors often know through life themes, and that people not directly impacted know about trauma through experiencing dilemmas in its communication (1998, p. 23). That is, as Davoine and Gaudillière (2004, p. xxvii) explain, "*a-letheia*," the "very name of truth," is synonymous with "non-forgetting." Whether or not people choose to know the massive traumatic event is inconsequential; they will hold on to the attempted wipe-out in all its truth and suffering. Below, they powerfully capture the impossibility of erasing "facts and people" from memory:

> Our work brings into existence zones of nonexistence wiped out by a powerful blow that actually took place. But whatever the measures chosen for erasing facts and people from memory, the erasures, even when perfectly programmed, only set in motion a memory that does not forget and that is seeking to be inscribed. In Greek, non-forgetting is, literally, *a-letheia*: this is the very name of truth, at stake in this specific memory as in the scientific approach. Hence we do not have to choose between the minute detail and the global fact. Sometimes a

fit of madness tells us more than all the news dispatches about the leftover facts that have no right to existence (Davoine & Gaudillière, 2004, p. xxvii).

Jewish Americans and the Holocaust

The development of a national identity is based on transmission of collective memory. Yet what is collective memory? How do subsequent generations continue to incorporate accounts of other people's past experiences into the narratives they construct as memory? In Maurice Halbwachs' (1992) work on this subject, he discusses how all memory is conceived within a social context. While identifications vary between groups, historical memory is adjusted and transmitted within groups in order to advance the present needs and desires of its members (Halbwachs, 1992). That is, historical memories are shaped by a social framework that is relevant to the present time. For example, Halbwachs (1992) elucidates that the story of Massada, based on a battle between the Roman army and Jewish revolutionaries in 73 A.D., did not receive much attention or significance in Jewish history for almost 2,000 years. However, it gained value for Palestinian Jews in the 1920's, as it became a key symbol of military heroism and unwavering loyalty, and a courageous declaration of "resistance and resilience" (Coser, 1992, p. 33). In this way, Halbwachs emphasizes the selective assimilation of historical memories into present identities (1992).

In his article entitled, "The American National Narrative of the Holocaust: There Isn't Any," Novick (2003) discusses the absence of an American national statement about the Holocaust. Due to both geographical and psychological distance from events overseas, Novick (2003) suggests that America was not affected by the atrocity of the Holocaust in the same way as countries in Europe and Israel. Considering the devastation and destruction surrounding the Holocaust in Europe, he claims few non-Americans can truly understand its limited influence in America (Novick, 2003, p. 29). The American national narrative of World War II, he argues, relates to the widely recognized image of American soldiers triumphantly raising the flag on Iwo Jima, the shocking attack on Pearl Harbor, or the "mushroom cloud" over Hiroshima (2003, p. 29-30). Furthermore, while Europe witnessed an "absence which is a presence" following the extermination of most of its Jews, Americans experienced a mounting Jewish presence in society (Novick, 2003, p. 30). Thus, despite the fact that a growing number of states mandate teaching about the Holocaust in public schools and Holocaust museums are spreading nationwide, Novick (2003) concludes that the Holocaust is not a part of the collective national narrative.

Regarding an "American *Jewish* narrative" (Novick, 2003, p. 31), however, the development of the Holocaust as an integral part of its collective identity followed a similar pattern as that of its Israeli counterpart. Having considerably restricted the Holocaust from their awareness during the 1940s and 1950s, Americans underwent a transformation in subsequent decades which highlighted this collective trauma (Cole, 2002). Two reasons have been suggested for this change: first, the 1973 Yom Kippur War reminded Americans of Israel's vulnerability, and second, the Holocaust served as a symbol of unity, a "common denominator" for American Jews (Novick, 1999, p. 7). Novick (1999) further suggests that Americans' marginalization of the Holocaust until this time was less about the survivors' inhibition of memory than about Jewish-American leaders' attempts at assimilation. Indeed, the survivors' silence and the societal suppression of perceived weakness in favor of attempted "normalcy" were identical to that of the young Israel.

Cole's (2002) question of "use versus abuse" of Holocaust history in American society traces the entrance of the Holocaust into popular culture, specifically through the movie *Schindler's List* (p. 129). He discusses the terms "exceptionalist" and "constructivist," first proposed by Mintz (2001) to distinguish between two divergent approaches in depicting the Holocaust (Cole, 2002, p. 130). The "exceptionalist" voice in Holocaust studies views the Holocaust as a defining moment in history that requires a staunch and blunt telling of events (Cole, 2002). The "constructivist" suggests that even an event as extraordinary as the Holocaust must be understood through pre-existing categories that capture history in a manner appropriate for a specific audience (Cole, 2002). These opposing methods summarize an ongoing controversy regarding how to fairly discuss and depict the Holocaust in modern-day society. Indeed, we continue to grapple with the incomprehensible.

Doneson (1996) clearly struggles with the constructivist approach:

> Therefore, in American fiction films and films for television that deal with the Holocaust, it is necessary to

revert to American symbols and language in order to convey a comprehensible, Americanized perception of the (European) Holocaust. Among the identifying characteristics common to American commercial film are the much maligned soap opera format and the happy, upbeat ending. Are these traits suitable for dramatization of the Holocaust, or do they tend to trivialize the attempted genocide of European Jewry? (p. 71).

As Doneson (1996) herself asserts, writers such as Lawrence Langer find this "upbeat" representation to be in stark contrast to the "reality of doom" surrounding the Holocaust (p. 71). Yet, regardless of this inconsistency, any attempt to grasp the unknowable will inevitably fail to capture the actual event. Doneson (1996) asks, "Is it necessary to ready oneself for sadness in preparation for a visit to Auschwitz? Should one take snapshots of the gas chambers and crematoria? Is this a trivialization?" (p. 72). She concludes that "It is indeed a daily occurrence, though one whose purpose, presumably, is meant to be noble—an attempt to fathom the nightmare of Auschwitz" (Doneson, 1996, p. 72). Even Claude Lanzmann's *Shoah*, which attempts to "penetrate forbidden territory," must do so within the confines of media: "More than explaining history, Lanzmann wants to grasp it, to live it, to enter into it. But he cannot. And how many others are even willing to try?" That is, memories cannot capture the actual truth, and commemorations cannot depict historical events as they were (Doneson, 1996, p. 76). Perhaps the most we can hope for is a continued identification with Holocaust memories, an ongoing meeting between ourselves and our history.

Shoshana Felman (Felman & Laub, 1992) captures Lanzmann's position as the "creator" of *Shoah*, addressing his "triple role as the narrator of the film ... as the interviewer of the witnesses ... and as the inquirer" of the testimonies (p. 216). While Lanzmann serves as the sole continuous voice throughout the movie, Felman describes the ways in which he succeeds in taking himself entirely out of it by speaking solely what he hears and refraining from communicating his own perspective (Felman & Laub, 1992). This "silent" narration allows the accounts to be told by others, and indeed the stories "speak for themselves" (Felman & Laub, 1992, p. 218). In a sense, the absence of a storyteller creates space for bystanders of the atrocities to share their personal anecdotes.

At the same time, Felman (1992) does not intend to say that the interviewer remains silent or separates himself from the dialogue. Instead, Lanzmann engulfs himself in concrete, specific questions, entirely reversing the barrier of silence surrounding the enormity of the Holocaust through "small steps," or "concrete particulars" (Felman & Laub, 1992, p. 219). Yet, most striking about Felman's description of the narrator's role is his strength as an "echo"; while many witnesses worked to evade, reject, or simply ignore Lanzmann's questions, "the narrator is precisely there to insure that the question, in its turn, will go on" ((Felman & Laub, 1992, p. 221). That is, Lanzmann serves as an eyewitness to the question he posed and the frequent disconnect between the inquiry and the response (Felman & Laub, 1992, p. 221).

Felman writes, it "is the story of the liberation of the testimony through its desacralization; the story of the decanonization of the Holocaust for the sake of its previously impossible historicization" (Felman & Laub, 1992, p. 219). As the struggle for the "liberation of the testimony" continues, the lives of second, third, and fourth generations of survivors unfold in a world distinct from, yet forever linked to, the Holocaust. Neusner's (1973) belief that the second generation of Holocaust survivors exists in a more "complicated" world than the survivors themselves is debatable, but driven precisely by the awareness of the Holocaust's imprint and the way it has been inextricably woven into Jewish identity. Neusner writes of the second generation:

> They know about events, but have not experienced them. And what they know they perceive through their experience of a very different world. The story that gives meaning and imparts transcendence to the everyday experiences of being Jewish simply does not correspond to the reality of the generations born since 1945 (Neusner, 1973, p. 296).

The Incorporation of the Holocaust in Israeli Identity

Since the emergence of the State of Israel, the place of Holocaust memories in its national narrative has been controversial and inconsistent. Arad (2003) recognizes the Holocaust as "a double-edged taboo; often in juxtaposition with one another, it was regarded on the one hand as

CHAPTER ONE

'uncanny' and 'dangerous,' and on the other hand as 'sacred' and 'consecrated'" (p. 5) Bar-On (1995) describes an atmosphere in 1950's Israel in which Holocaust emotions were unwarranted and rebuffed. Indeed, the catastrophe of the Holocaust seemed to clash with the bold identity of the *Sabras*[2] and the emerging Zionistic identity based on independence, self-sufficiency, and strength: "It was believed that beginning anew in a sovereign Jewish state would result in a 'normalized' existence for the Jews, provided this catastrophic history, as epitomized by the *Shoah*, would be plowed under" (Arad, 2003, p. 7). Silence regarding past trauma was therefore promoted, out of fear that any recognition of past struggle would undermine the current quest for a "normal" existence. It was perhaps unsurprising that survivors—plagued by their traumatic experiences and filled with guilt that they survived while others did not—adhered to the notion of silence as a solution (Arad, 2003). Thus, the Holocaust was restricted from becoming part of the Israelis' modern collective consciousness. As survivor and writer Aharon Appelfeld is quoted as saying:

> The first years in Israel were years of repression and denial, of constructing a personality with no trace of what you went through and who you were ... The inner world was suppressed, as if it did not exist; it shrunk and sunk into deep sleep ... Whoever survived and came here brought with him much silence. It was tacitly accepted not to speak about certain matters and not to touch certain wounds (Arad, 2003, p. 7).

Langer (1991) places the Israeli response within a larger scope, suggesting that Westerners struggle to understand situations which are somehow outside of man's control.

> The concept of "you cannot do nothing" is so alien to the self-reliant Western mind (dominated by the idea of the individual as *agent* of his fate) that its centrality, its *blameless* centrality to the camp experience continues to leave one morally disoriented. The very principle of

---

[2] Native-born Israelis.

blameless inaction by former victims is foreign to the ethical premises of our culture, where we sometimes confuse such inaction with cowardice, self-indulgence, or indifference (Langer, 1991, p. 85).

Unfortunately, the societal disavowal of the realities of the Holocaust was a powerful trend. In a 1952 article entitled "Israeli Culture and Society," Samuel Koenig describes the "patterns of life" among the Jewish community of Palestine; the trends he considers "most important" include "socialism, the glorification of the laborer and labor, pioneerism (*halutziut*), Westernism, secularism, and democracy" (Koenig, 1952, p. 160). No mention is made of the Holocaust, and survivors remain altogether unidentified within the larger category of "immigrants." Koenig does, however, comment that many of these immigrants arrived "psychically scarred and physically weakened," but only as indication that the immigrants "show little, if any, inclination or ability to become pioneers, to go on the land, or to engage in other difficult but necessary tasks" (Koenig, 1952, p. 165). Such an obvious disregard of Holocaust experience and survival, while shocking to read today, was unremarkable and, in fact, encouraged at the time. It was not until the circumstantial arrival of war criminal Adolf Eichmann in Israel in 1961-1962, the 1967 Six-Day War, and the 1973 Yom Kippur War, that Israelis began to integrate the realities of their recent past.

Numerous changes occurred in Israel between the 1940s and 1970s, and survivors' experiences were slowly but increasingly tolerated. Politically, the Eichmann trial was an unplanned eye-opener for Israeli society: as a public trial in which survivors were asked to testify, opportunity was created for Israeli citizens to listen to horrifying and heartbreaking life stories for the first time (Arad, 2003). Immediately, the Holocaust was transformed from a message endorsing "Zionist" philosophy to a trauma of real individuals (Arad, 2003, p. 12). The younger generation was particularly moved by these accounts and began to identify with survivors' past suffering (Arad, 2003, p. 12). As Tom Segev writes in his comprehensive book, *The Seventh Million* (1991), "The trial of Adolf Eichmann served as therapy for the nation, starting a process of identification with the tragedy of the victims and survivors, a process that continues to this day" (p. 11). Furthermore, accompanying the identification with Holocaust survivors was the internalization of what

Arad (2003) calls "holocaustal anxiety" and Solomon (1993) labels "existential anxiety"—Israelis' belief that the threat of extermination was real at any moment of vulnerability. During the 1967 Six-Day War, this sentiment established a widespread terror that losing the war might mean the end of the Jewish people. Victory represented defeat of both current and past enemies. Finally, the impact of the 1973 Yom Kippur War further consolidated the integration of past and present: Israelis experienced first-hand what it was like to be caught off guard, to feel defenseless and out of control, to undergo extensive loss (Arad, 2003, p. 16). The seemingly stark contrast between Holocaust survivors and non-survivors was dimmed.

Bar-Tal (2001) further discusses the crucial role of fear in Israeli society, and identifies fear as easily overriding hope because it occurs "automatically" and "unconsciously," and is fueled by past experiences (p. 605). Bar-Tal writes about the current Middle Eastern conflict when he says, "The society provides the contexts, information, models, emphases, and instructions that influence the emotions of its members" (Bar-Tal, 2001, p. 605). However, this social basis of emotion is also descriptive of the influence of fear on Israel's early rejection of and identification with Holocaust survivors. In a dramatic attempt to start "new" and be "normal," *Sabras* struggled to bridge the gap between a past full of fear, shame, and humiliation, and a present filled with hope, pride, and strength. The fragile identity of the young nation was at risk of further fragmentation by the victims. As Langer (1991) writes of Holocaust victims,

> Self-esteem is crucial to the evolution of heroic memory; the narratives in these testimonies reflect a partially traumatized or maimed self-esteem, lingering like a non-fatal disease without cure. Heroic memory is virtually unavailable to such witnesses, because for them remembering is invariably associated with a jumbled terminology and morality that confuse staying alive with the intrepid will to survival (p. 176).

Davoine and Gaudillière (2004) reaffirm the human need for control when they write, "it is better to assume that one is oneself the cause of an inexplicable event, or to unload it onto the other, than to confront an event without a reason." (p. 72). Fear of the unknown is the most crippling of all.

With the negative impacts of fear aside, Bar-Tal (2001) elucidates a number of positive consequences of fear in stressful situations: it encourages groups to prepare for danger, it calls attention to cues that suggest impending threat, it enhances unity among group members, and it pushes people to act in support of the group (p. 609). As Holocaust narratives were incorporated into Israelis' identities, and the contagion of fear evolved out of political and historical tumult, group identity simultaneously flourished. Today, the communication and transmission of these fears can be pinpointed in Israeli media, art, literature, and politics. As Segev writes,

> The Seventh Million concerns the ways in which the bitter events of the past continue to shape the life of a nation. Just as the Holocaust imposed a posthumous collective identity on its six million victims, so too it formed the collective identity of this new country—not just for the survivors who came after the war but for all Israelis, then and now. This is why I have called them the seventh million (1991, p. 11).

Combat and Loss, Solidarity and Pride

Parallel to the collective sense of fear, the continuous political chaos, and the quest for a common narrative, Israeli pride evolved. Combat in and of itself served to enhance Israelis' solidarity by uniting their efforts around a mutual cause: the survival of the State of Israel. Even amongst authors who focus on the difficulty of inscribing one's traumatic past within the present, combat is recognized as a powerful source of integration: "Combat evokes in those who are fighting side by side a passion for taking care of the other physically and psychically, equivalent to the earliest and deepest family relationships ... For the bond of combat erases the distinction between oneself and the other" (Davoine & Gaudillière, 2004, p. 154-155). In Israel, the placement of military cemeteries inside and alongside civil cemeteries symbolizes the rallying around a "military community" (Weiss, 1997, p. 92) and the creation of a familial atmosphere. Soldiers continue to be viewed as the "silver platter" which makes Israelis' lives possible, and thus receive the highest form of respect and appreciation (Solomon, 1993, p. 251).

From this standpoint, it is unimportant whether "oneself" and "other" have faced similar or divergent life experiences, so long as they work together towards a current, common goal. Amongst Holocaust survivors as well, active involvement in a mutual cause seems to have the potential for additional reparatory effects in terms of the reestablishment of agency and the mending of a wounded identity. For example, in the case of "Nathan A.," "Still a teenager at the end of the war, he made his way to Israel, fought in its many wars, was wounded, but clearly reclaimed some of his lost dignity by actively participating in a common effort in behalf of Jewish freedom" (Langer, 1991, p. 137). On the other hand, as revealed in the case of "Alex H.," the effect of combat is illusory in that it establishes "a paradox of his post-Holocaust life: he is unhappy that this should have made him happy. There is, he now realizes, no vindication, no connection, no compensation for the state to which circumstances reduced him during those years" (Langer, 1991, p. 145). In other words, present combat cannot undo past trauma, but might assist to some extent in the renewal of one's agency and the reestablishment of oneself as a "dignified," "active" human being (Langer, 1991).

In a study examining the development of identity via projective drawings of Palestinian and Israeli Arab children in the West Bank and Gaza, Elbedour, Bastien, and Center (1997) differentiate between three levels of identity: 1) "individualized/personal identity" (where the self is "I"-centered), 2) "cultural identity" (where the self is characterized by the collective "we"), and 3) "conflict/political identity" (where the self is integrated along themes of "us-them") (p. 221). Results revealed that "the children raised in the greatest conflict identify most with the conflict while the children raised in relative peace are more likely to depict an individuated personal identity" (Elbedour et al, 1997, p. 225). Although this study did not include any Jewish-Israeli children, this finding is relevant in terms of collective identity and trauma, as it speaks to the tangled relationship between conflicts, fears, and solidarity. Furthermore, in a country where group cohesion provides the individual with a greater sense of pride, Israel faces the challenge of concurrently fostering individual tasks and needs. Reminiscent of Alex H.'s misconception that fighting for a common cause might undo his past circumstances (Langer, 1991), combat alone cannot do the work of "working through" and the necessary integration of past and present.

Beyond the act of combat, "bereavement and commemoration" of those killed in war is a key promoter of national solidarity (Weiss, 1997, p. 92). Weiss (1997) identifies a sort of "cult of the fallen" in Israeli society, where death is idealized as a heroic sacrifice (p. 91). Weiss points out that Israel's Remembrance Day—the memorial day for soldiers killed in combat—takes place exactly seven days following Holocaust Memorial Day and one day prior to Israel's Independence Day; thus, she elucidates a national narrative that leads "from destruction (holocaust) via sacrifice (the fallen) to salvation (independence)" (Weiss, 1997, p. 92). Furthermore, as the implementation of Remembrance Day proceedings targets the entire population, "it transforms the whole nation into one bereaved family" (Weiss, 1997, p. 93). The sense of family and communal mourning is intensely unifying, and reflects a community sitting Shiva together on a national level. Coser (1992), as well, argued that people do not remember historical events directly, but rather "history can only be stimulated in indirect ways through reading or listening or in commemoration and festive occasions when people gather together to remember in common the deeds and accomplishments of long-departed members of the group" (p. 24).

Zahava Solomon, who served in the Israeli Defense Forces as head of the Research Branch in the Medical Corps for over a decade, discusses the concept of "reactivation" of trauma that occurs through repeated wars (1993, p. 189). In her analyses on combat stress reaction (CSR), formerly known as shell shock, Solomon found that one CSR reaction frequently signifies impending CSR reactions in future wars. That is, current trauma does not "heal" past trauma; rather, it "deepens" it (Solomon, 1993, p. 209, quoting Berman, 1985). This effect extends to the second generation of Holocaust survivors, although they did not personally witness the Holocaust. In a three-year longitudinal study, Solomon (1993) found that "the passage of time did not have the same healing effect on the PTSD of the second generation as on that of other soldiers" (p. 232); instead, the second generation maintained a heightened sensitivity to stress and to combat's damaging consequences (p. 233). More generally, offspring of survivors have been found to react with high levels of anxiety to various situations, displaying "high narcissistic vulnerability, survival guilt, and conflicts over the expression of aggression" (Solomon, 1993, p. 229). Indeed, the aftereffects of the Holocaust continue to manifest themselves on both personal and societal levels.

Segev quotes the editor in chief of *Maariv*[3] as asking, "'What will I say to my loved ones, my burned ones, my murdered ones when they come to me at night, and as they continue to come forever?'" (1991, p. 206). As his chapters trace history, beginning with "Hitler," "Holocaust," "Israel," and "Restitution: How Much Will We Get for Grandma and Grandpa?" Segev (1991) illuminates the inseparable connection of past, present, and future, and concludes his book with chapters entitled "Growing Up: From War to War" and "Memory: The Struggle to Shape the Past." He writes, "Israelis are obsessed with history. They are the offspring of a nation, a religion, and a culture that has dismissed the present and left the future in the hands of faith and fate. The past thus becomes an object of worship" (Segev, 1991, p. 513). This "obsession," he explains, remains forever linked to Israel's ongoing "need to justify—to the rest of the world, and to itself—its very right to exist" (p. 514). The Holocaust, Israel, and Jewish identity continuously blend in the collective narrative of Jews worldwide. This study therefore aims to examine the transmission of Holocaust trauma and memories amongst the third generation of survivors, in the hope that the present will no longer be "dismissed."

The Third Generation of the Holocaust

Over the past two decades, researchers and clinicians alike have grown curious about the impact of the Holocaust on the lives of its third generation descendants. Nevertheless, the literature regarding grandchildren of survivors remains sparse, and repeatedly points to "contradictory" hypotheses and conclusions yielded by pertinent studies in the field. While many inquiries trace the long-sensed and increasingly recognized intergenerational transmission of Holocaust trauma and memory (Felsen, 1998; Rubenstein, Cutter, & Templer, 1989-1990), others underscore survivors' and their offspring's "resilience in the face of adversity" (Sigal, 1998, p. 582). Although "resilience" rightfully honors the struggle and endurance of survivors and their descendants in a post-Holocaust world, it is often interpreted as an absence of Holocaust themes, sensitivities and reverberations in their day-to-day lives. For example, a number of

---

3   A popular daily newspaper published in Israel.

researchers suggest that the transgenerational transmission of trauma has altogether ceased by the third generation (Bachar, Cale, Eisenberg, & Dasberg, 1994). Such conclusions invite questions about the concept of intergenerational trauma and the apparent efforts to either prove or refute its existence; the hunt for psychopathology versus the pursuit of a broader psychodynamic understanding of the third generation experience; and the implications of tracing "trauma trails" (Atkinson, 2002) two generations following such horrors.

Inconsistent findings have been accounted for by differences in sample, procedure, measures, and other methodological details. In an attempt to "resolve the divergence of the clinical and non-clinical findings on intergenerational transmission of trauma, between qualitative and quantitative approaches, and between methodologically more robust versus less robust studies," Sagi-Schwartz, van IJzendoorn, and Bakermans-Kranenburg (2008, p. 106) conducted a meta-analysis of research on the third generation. However, despite their defined objective, Sagi-Schwartz et al (2008) excluded all qualitative publications from their investigation, noting that such studies "do not fit into a meta-analysis paradigm" (p. 111). Furthermore, they acknowledged their attempts to retain a more "homogenous" group by including only non-clinical samples, thereby allowing their findings to be more "robust" (Sagi-Schwartz et al, 2008, p. 111). Thus, their conclusion that "participants showed no evidence for tertiary traumatization in Holocaust survivor families" must once again be understood within the margins of their research questions and criterion (Sagi-Schwartz et al, 2008, p. 105). Sagi-Schwartz et al (2008) recognize at the start of their paper that "the field still seems to beg for further systematic examination of third generation effects..." (p. 107); indeed, with the completion of their work, this yearning persists.

Alongside others, Bar-On (2008) addresses the deductions of quantitative analyses such as those described above, emphasizing the ways in which these studies "undermine what voices within the second and third generations tell us, and the echoes these stories have within us" (p. ix). He elucidates the problem with the notion of "methodologically more robust" studies (Sagi-Schwartz et al, 2008, p. 106), impelling us to question whether or not such models exist; for example, Bar-On (2008) questions the concept of "control groups," often comprised of "families of Jewish European descent who did not live under Nazi occupation," as a contrast to experimental groups of Holocaust survivors and their offspring (p. xi). Specifically, he emphasizes that members of "control groups" may have fled from Nazi-controlled territories, lost family members and friends in the Holocaust, and themselves wrestled with a complex experience of bereavement:

> So, they go through processes of mourning, of silencing these losses, as they "have no right to feel effected" in the eyes of the survivors, or in their own eyes, and in my view therefore cannot be counted as a control group in any deeper psychological meaning (Bar-On, 2008, p. xi).

Bar-On further addresses the refutation of intergenerational trauma, linking this impulse to the shame and silence that surrounded one's identity as a Holocaust survivor during the emergence of the State of Israel (2008, p. x). That is, the persistence of this historically-rooted dynamic may motivate individuals to deny the ongoing impact of the Holocaust in an attempt to assimilate with the "normal" lifestyle and mentality of the collective consciousness surrounding them. In addition, Bar-On (2008) suggests that the disavowal of intergenerational trauma transmission may reflect researchers' apprehension about imposing an additional, multi-generational burden or responsibility on survivors. He states of these researchers:

> They may have reacted to the assumption that relational aftereffects can be seen as some kind of an accusation toward the survivors who suffered so much, who were stigmatized enough, that they should not be burdened with any unnecessary additional stigma. This approach puts the survivors' assumed needs to be protected above those of their children and grandchildren (Bar-On, 2008, p. x).

Yet, what is the value of "protecting" survivors from recognizing the long-lasting impact of their traumatic experiences? Litvak-Hirsch and Bar-On (2006) depict grandchildren's increased opportunity to achieve "psychological freedom," particularly through their unique ability to address "undiscussable" themes within their families (p. 475). In doing so, these grandchildren are able to initiate new narrative possibilities amongst family members, breaking down the "double wall" of silence (Bar-On, 1995, p. 20) created by survivors and their children. Furthermore, the needs of the third generation are highlighted in *Echoes of the Trauma*, which explores the second generation's upbringing by survivor parents as well as survivors' children's experience of parenting their own adolescent children (Wiseman & Barber, 2008). While Wiseman and Barber (2008) emphasize the ways in which the second generation's "quest to heal the echoes of the parental past is a powerful motivator for generational change," they simultaneously recognize that amending one's "intergenerational transmission of problematic parenting" is not a simple pursuit (p. 227). They describe a conflictual scenario between a second generation parent and her third generation adolescent child, noting: "In some cases the communication was portrayed as more open through their parents' eyes than through the adolescent's eyes, perhaps representing the gap between the parents' explicit attitudes and actual behavior" (Wiseman & Barber, 2008, p. 226).

Regardless of awareness or intent, therefore, residues of the Holocaust persist. Scharf (2007) examined whether grandchildren of Holocaust survivors differed from a comparison group during the transition period in which adolescent males depart home to enter a three year compulsory military service in the Israel Defense Force (IDF). Findings revealed that boys whose parents were both offspring of survivors reported a less positive sense of self and perceived their parents as "less accepting and less encouraging independence" (Scharf, 2003, p. 603). In addition, a measure given to their peers indicated that sons of two second generation parents showed "inferior emotional, instrumental, and social functioning" (Scharf, 2007, p. 617-618). Scharf concluded: "It is recommended that researchers and clinicians develop awareness of the possible traces of trauma in the second and the third generation despite their sound functioning in their daily lives" (2007, p. 603).

As a follow up to Scharf's (2007) study, Berant and Hever (in press) focused on granddaughters of the Holocaust from their maternal side. Berant and Hever (in press) explored three non-clinical samples of young women facing distinct stages of separation-individuation: the draft to the IDF and the accompanying separation from their families, the transition to first-time motherhood, and the group voyage to concentration camps in Poland. Of particular significance were their discrepant findings based on the type of measure utilized; that is, when relying on self-report measures, Berant and Hever (in press) discovered that granddaughters of survivors did not endorse struggling more than their counterparts during these life changes. However, in an attempt to capture internal mental representations by asking granddaughters to describe their mothers in writing, for example, they found that women at all three stages showed "less positive maternal representations than the control group"; specifically, these women revealed "more ambivalence" towards their mothers, who "were perceived as less benevolent and less ambitious" (Berant & Hever, in press, p. 17). In reflecting on the inconsistencies in their own findings, Berant and Hever note, "…at a more subtle level, one can trace the distant influences of their grandparents that have led to specific dynamics among the third generation and between daughters and mothers" (in press, p. 26). Imparted in their study is the awareness that "Perhaps open, exploratory questions about these issues would be useful here" (Berant & Hever, in press, p. 22).

From a perspective of health, Chaitin (2003) investigated how families contend with and work through their history by exploring the coping styles amongst two or three generations of 20 families of Holocaust survivors. Utilizing and advancing Danieli's (1988) classification of post-war adaptation, Chaitin (2003) identified six distinct coping patterns exhibited by her participants, categorizing them as: "victim families," "fighter families," "those who made it," "numb families," "life goes on," and "split families" (p. 305). Chaitin's (2003) life-story interviews revealed that coping styles, as well, are transmitted to and incorporated by family members across generations. In the realm of psychopathology, Fossion, Rejas, Servais, Pelc, and Hirsch (2003) identified a direct relationship between the trauma experienced by survivors and the psychiatric symptoms developed by their grandchildren two generations later. Specifically, they described the thwarting of the developmental process in an atmosphere of silence, as the grandchildren they encountered in their clinical work lacked a historical root that might provide context for their parents' way of being: "Due to the impossibility of referring to past experience, these families were continually confronted with new situations at each stage of life – particularly when facing issues of separation and independence, thus generating an insurmountable crisis" (Fossion et al, 2003, p. 523).

In the best case scenario, grandchildren of survivors are able to recognize the intergenerational patterns at play, utilizing words to metabolize their emotional experiences, and integrating their knowledge of historical traumas with present manifestations of past suffering. When this does not occur, however, traumas are "paradoxically re-created" generation after generation, with or without conscious awareness (Talby-Abarbanel, 2011, p. 230). In her case presentation of a third generation survivor named "Ann," Talby-Abarbanel (2011) captures the incessant enactments that occur in the face of unspoken and unspeakable grief and loss. Ann is first described as wrestling with "un-integrated" parts of herself without a framework for the origin of such disintegration (Talby-Abarbanel, 2011, p. 219). While confronting her mother about their tormented relationship, Ann learns of her Holocaust history for the very first time; she is subsequently able to comprehend the root of her past obsession with Holocaust books and films, her lifelong creations of artwork centered on themes of relocation and isolation, and her vivid, complex dreams of "separateness" and "attachment" (Talby-Abarbanel, 2011, p. 233). Talby-Abarbanel writes:

> Ann added that by avoiding the trauma and by refraining from working it through, they [her parents] paradoxically re-created the same atmosphere in their own family, from which she now needed to distance herself. Indigestible non-verbal terror, unbearable pain, and apocalyptic fantasies were always in the air (2011, p. 230).

Having a place to explore and symbolize their experience (whether through psychotherapy or through open-ended interviews such as those conducted in this study) therefore allows third generation survivors to promote connection and growth within their families, to discover words that might heal the torment of unexpressed emotions and dynamics, and to honor their history while re-working its previously debilitating impact on generation after generation.

Bar-On (2008) relays a personal experience with a student in one of his workshops, who claimed disbelief about the concept of a "second generation" of the Holocaust despite her technically belonging within this group (p. x). Bar-On (2008) recalls the impassioned responses of this woman's peers, who understandably felt their own experiences contested by her bold, dismissive statement. The disagreements within the field of third generation Holocaust research elicit reactions of parallel intensity, highlighting the personal investment and far-reaching implication of these studies to the individuals conducting them. Bar-On writes: "The ambivalence of researchers in this domain can be understood, as we study a complex phenomenon many years after the original occurrences, effected by several simultaneous processes" (2011, p. xi). Yet, as the grandchildren of survivors are continually motivated to confront their parents' and grandparents' experiences, to articulate multifaceted narratives, and to pursue an intergenerational perspective at once removed from and connected to the Holocaust, it has become increasingly imperative for their traumas to be acknowledged and their voices to be heard.

CHAPTER 2: RESEARCH APPROACH

My life story extends beyond the conscious and the verbal. It has always entailed both the things I said and those that I would not, or could not, articulate. Alongside my family, I reacted to my history for years—whether through unwarranted fear, displaced paranoia, or exaggerated experiences of loss—but struggled to describe the entry of the past in my present life. As I initiated this work, I reflected on the silent communications, unspoken truths, and implicit attitudes that accompany my family identity and continually influence its dynamics. A literature review then provided the long-awaited and desired words to describe the capacities and failures of language in depicting traumatic experience. Upon inviting other third generation survivors to engage in the present interviews, I wondered how spoken and unspoken elements of their accounts, as well, might provide a glimpse into history. Thus, as this "research" got underway and "hypotheses" were set in place, I anticipated that powerful Holocaust themes, emotions, and enactments would direct the course of these interviews. The "data," I assumed, would (for lack of a better term) "speak" for itself.

Ten Jewish women between the ages of 21 and 31 were interviewed in this work; seven identified as "American" and three identified as "half-Israeli, half-American." Clearly in search of mutuality and commonality, I chose to focus solely on women in order to more comprehensively explore the granddaughters' experiences. Participants were recruited from universities and synagogues on the East Coast[1] by word of mouth, having been informed that the interviews would explore the ways in which historical events may have impacted their families and intergenerational developments may relate to their personal identities. Dozens of women promptly and enthusiastically responded to this introductory description of the interviews. The first ten women to express interest and availability were then scheduled for a meeting. A number of the participants later relayed their interview experience to friends, furthering the interest in this work and leading others to contact me in hopes of arranging an

---

1 All names and locations have been changed to maintain the confidentiality of the participants.

interview. Finally, a couple of participants contacted me following our meeting to express their appreciation for the experience and to request a copy of their interview transcript. The urge to share their narratives and reflect on their histories seemed profound, and I was left feeling that these encounters provided a timely, highly desired outlet that many had previously lacked.

Each interview was conducted by me and consisted of one 60- to 120-minute session, depending on the scope of the narrative. All interviews began with my open-ended statement, "Tell me about yourself," as was done by Ewing (2004) in her studies. The conversations then took the form of psychoanalytic interviews, in which I remained as minimalist as possible in my interventions and used my free associations in reaction to the interviewee. Most women spoke fluently and eagerly throughout the interview; however, if a participant remained relatively unresponsive or limited in the depth of her narrative, I posed specific questions in order to stimulate the conversation, keeping the following questions in mind: Who is this person? How does she identify herself? What does she know about her family history? What does she not know and why? Where does she come from? How does that affect her? What is her role within her family? How do the limitations of her knowledge impact her experience? How might she know more? This approach was selected in order to encourage participants to speak openly and freely about their Holocaust history, and to allow me to respond to the content and mood of their stories as well as to my own reactions to the narratives.

Topics of interest that arose in these interviews included the following: In what ways has the Holocaust affected their feminine identities? What are some of their feelings and fantasies related to having a family and being a mother? How do they plan to raise their children similarly to or differently from the ways they were raised? Do they have any recurring dreams or recent nightmares that they recall? Do they have a tendency to avoid talking about certain topics or specific situations? Do they experience any difficulties sleeping or concentrating? How much of an authoritarian figure was present in their family growing up? How much were they permitted to know about their family history? How much were they allowed to feel? Do they report any experiences of fear, helplessness, guilt, shame, humiliation, or expectation of death? Are they frequently agitated, anxious, or angry? While many of these questions were answered throughout the course of the interviews, I posed them directly when I felt there was more to explore on any given topic. At times, my direct questioning was met with hesitation, rejection, or a discreet evasion of the subject matter at hand; in this way, the interviews exposed how the Holocaust has been handled by members of the third generation by tapping into the deep unconscious structures of participants through their use of language, or lack thereof.

Following each interview, I kept a log of my own thoughts, associations, and reactions to the participants' narratives, as well as any feelings or observations that arose during and after the interview. This log served to both keep track of the ideas that were developed throughout the course of the interviews and to engage with my unconscious. The interviews thus became a dynamic event—a process—that explored features of both the transference and countertransference. Furthermore, my exploration was informed by the literature of Packer and Addison (1989) and Josselson, Lieblich, and and McAdams (2003), who maintain that underlying narrative research is the belief that human nature cannot be captured by a single theory, much like text analysis cannot be encapsulated by one person's perspective or interpretation. As Packer and Addison explain, "Interpretive research emphasizes that the researcher must *not* act as if he or she is a value-free researcher who can objectively see things as they 'really' are, or that the 'data' collected is, in some way, independent of the person who collects it" (1989, p. 42). Instead, throughout the interview process, the researcher should bear in mind, "I was the one who was taking notes, asking questions in the interview, and selecting what aspects of documents and literature were significant for my purposes" (Packer & Addison, 1989, p. 41). Thus, these interviews represent the spoken and unspoken elements of communication and understanding between two individual people.

In drawing conclusions from the data, I utilized a thematic analysis to examine the emergent themes, both in the actual interviews and in my own reactions to the narratives, which signified responses to Holocaust trauma. I looked for recurring ideas, for metaphors that evoked particular images, and for words that seemed laden with meaning. I also made a point of focusing on both explicit and implicit information—including pauses, repetitions, slips of the tongue, hesitations, laughter, tears, and tone of voice. Hence, the "data" by definition encompassed both verbal and non-verbal features of the narrative. While this method allowed for layers of meaning to emerge, the complexity of analyzing non-verbal aspects of verbal accounts was also the greatest obstacle inherent in this approach. For example, differentiating between what was purposely left unsaid and what was unconsciously avoided was not always possible. Ultimately, however, within an unencumbered space that welcomed words, silences, and everything in between, these women's life stories began to unfold.

CHAPTER 3: BETHANY

> Recently both of them have been talking about things more, especially my grandfather, because I guess as they get older they want to make sure we remember everything.

In the case of a massive collective trauma like the Holocaust, the transmission of memories and autobiographical information shifts from the individual to the communal. As can be seen in the above quote by a 22-year-old, third generation Holocaust descendant named Bethany[1], individual experience has entirely transformed into collective memory. After all, it is not simply that Bethany was told a story that she is expected to "remember"; it is far beyond a story, and yet it has never been told. One might expect the offspring of survivors to have been infused with rich and detailed accounts of their grandparents' experiences in order for memory to persist. However, in the aftermath of this massive trauma, immense and lasting pain has solicited silence and secrecy over verbal communication. Perhaps not surprisingly, these silences engender the most powerful messages of suffering and an unmistakable cry for help from future generations.

Bethany definitively states, "...they want to make sure we remember everything," as though Bethany and her siblings were present during the Holocaust to create the memory in the first place. Yet, she did not live during the Holocaust, and neither did her siblings. So, how does she continue to "remember"? The post-Holocaust phrase to "never forget" and the Israeli national song "If I forget thee Jerusalem, forget my right hand" immediately come to mind. Like Bethany, Kaplan (1996) speaks to the transmission of memories to future generations:

> When a Holocaust survivor brings a child into the world, she is looking to the child for a second chance at life.

---

[1] All names and other identifying details have been changed throughout to maintain the confidentiality of the participants.

> She is hoping to shelter her child from the atrocities she suffered. However, in most cases, the shelter of silence becomes a Holocaust monument that casts its shadows over the life of her child (p. 218).

As future generations continue to carry the historical trauma, they serve as memory receptacles for a past they did not experience, and are left to testify as to what happened to their ancestors.

Thus, trauma is transmitted intergenerationally, and can be observed through various life patterns, including dietary, relational, and religious decisions; a general attitude towards the world marked by excessive guilt, fear, and the expectation of death; and a devotion of one's life to an ever-present, unspoken story that must be reconstructed like pieces of a puzzle. That is, amidst debilitating silences and deeply rooted family secrets, third generation Holocaust survivors attempt to construct the foundation of a narrative for their predecessors, and indirectly for themselves. It seems that entire generations are unknowingly devoted to this task; specifics regarding who exactly does the work are secondary. After all, past traumas persist until they have been worked through, and the "unthought known" (Bollas, 1989) drives the life of a third generation survivor until the seeds of awareness are planted and mourning has begun.

Constructing a Narrative in Silence and Absence

"It's just like how you know... you know those are your parents. I've always known my grandparents are Holocaust survivors." Bethany does not recall learning about the Holocaust, nor can she pinpoint a time when she realized that this was her history. The knowledge has simply always been present, like knowing that her parents are her parents. Indirectly, Bethany speaks to the immense work that has gone into uncovering some historical truth within her family's implicit collusion of silence: "I've always known that my grandparents are Holocaust survivors and I don't know how I know that... I don't know. It's just stuff I guess we've gathered or that have come into my head..." The "stuff" she has "gathered" is a jumble of knowledge, made up of concrete information that she has heard, read, and learned, and, more frequently, intangible data that have "come into" her head through associations, feelings, and reactions to silence. Thus, her family secrets exist as an "unthought known":

> B: She had one brother and I've never met him, I've never heard anything about him. They don't speak about him. My grandmother will not like it I think if we ask...
> N: You've asked her?
> B: We've asked her and we've asked my grandpa, who stayed the same... just silent. And for the most part, what we think and what my dad thinks, too... he grew up never knowing his uncle. I think he knew he had an uncle, but that was it. And no one ever spoke of him. And what my dad and mom both tell me is that they think he married someone non-Jewish and went back to France and lives there. I don't even know if he's still alive, but... which is crazy.
> N: How do you think your dad knew that there was an uncle?
> B: I have no idea, I think through pictures... I don't even know if they had anything. But I'm assuming it was just like a picture or something. Because I don't even know... the reason I know... I mean, I feel like I've always known.

Most often, the source of Bethany's knowledge is unclear; thus, a linear, coherent narrative is absent. However, the power of the knowledge remains, like the weight of a silence that cannot be described yet reliably transmits information. Similarly, in attempting to describe her grandparents' nightmares and her father's attempt to communicate this childhood experience, Bethany states:

> I vaguely remember him saying something like, "It was really hard to wake up at night to hear your parents screaming." So, that's obviously something that stuck in my head. But I don't really ever remember him ever telling me that. And I don't know if I read that somewhere... that Holocaust survivors do that... or if that actually did happen. But I think that he's told me that. I just don't

know if he wants to talk about it or... so we just don't.

Bethany's attempt to share an interaction with her father provides a compelling example of the muddle surrounding the transmission of traumatic memory. In a sense, Bethany is asking: Was this memory spoken or read? I think I heard this from my dad, but did the conversation actually happen? How and when and why did it happen? If we spoke, does that mean we can talk about it again? Or maybe the haziness of the memory is a sign that we shouldn't?

Ironically, this jumble of knowledge indicates the beginning of narrative formation. As Bethany attempts to reflect on what she knows, how she knows it, and in what way this relates to the rest of her family's knowledge, there is an increasing desire to know more:

> So the things that I don't say I probably don't know the answers to, but... I don't know, some I might just leave out so you can ask me. But I think because I have never asked him, which I probably should sit down one day and ask him, I just don't know a lot of the things... I just hear.

As Bethany discloses her family's history to a curious interviewer with a curiosity much like her own, the gaps in her knowledge continue to unfold. At points, Bethany's partaking in her family's silence is striking: "But I think because I have never asked him, which I probably should sit down one day and ask him..." Nonetheless, she has succeeded in acquiring a great deal of knowledge, and has become a source of information in her family, particularly for her father. Her willingness to engage with their traumatic past and wonder about both the presence and absence of information allows Bethany to begin working through this past trauma.

Bethany goes on to describe the failure of language in depicting her grandfather's experience:

> My grandfather used to talk about his friends from camp and I thought they were his friends from summer camp... and only like, really, within the past five years did it click in my head... he never went to camp. He was in concentration camp. And I didn't know that growing up. But I

mean I knew he was in a concentration camp, I've known my whole life that my grandfather had numbers on his arm, but it never crossed my mind when he would talk about his friends from camp, you know? He never ever spoke about anything when I was growing up, and my dad knows nothing. And he always says... my dad was in summer camp and I guess a bunch of his friends had parents that were Holocaust survivors and they asked him on *Tisha B'av*[2] to stand up and tell a little bit and he said he just didn't know that much to tell because his parents never spoke about it. Now he's learning a little bit more and he asks me questions because I'm probably the one who knows about it the most in our family.

The above narrative highlights a number of issues. First, Bethany has taken on the role of narrator, and thus of caretaker, in her family. In a sense, her quest for knowledge reassures her father, "It's okay to wonder. We will not kill my grandparents with our curiosity." Thus, Bethany reacts differently to the familial silence. While she abides by the implicit family agreement not to ask, she nevertheless opens the door by what she calls an "interest" in history. Bethany explains her role by stating, "I wanted to know so much more." That is, her ability to become curious simultaneously infuses her with the strength to heal. Ultimately, Bethany's attempt to bridge the gap between the past and the present encourages her ancestors, "It's okay to rejoin the world." Secondly, Bethany's grandfather did not go to summer camp, but Bethany's father did, as did Bethany. In a sense, Bethany's summer camp experiences and associations to summer camp evokes the idea, "I'll go to the right kind of camp that you were supposed to go to as well." That is, Bethany is beginning to work through her grandfather's past trauma partly by compensating for his experiences concretely.

Finally, Bethany's struggle with the word "camp" emphasizes the incomprehensibility of the Holocaust in a post-Holocaust world. In Bethany's attempt to make sense of an unfathomable experience using everyday language, she finds herself hitting a wall time and again; this

---

2 The ninth day of the month of Av in the Hebrew calendar is a day of mourning that is honored by fasting. This day commemorates the destruction of the First and Second Temples in Jerusalem.

reveals the obscenity of attempting to understand or convey the atrocities of the Holocaust. For example, she struggles to describe her late great-uncle's return to his living quarters at the end of the day, stating, "He came home... he came back to the barrack with the yellow band on his uniform." Indeed, there is no way for Bethany or anyone who has never lived in that kind of barrack to comprehend what this experience was like, and how it translates into a world where people come home at the end of their work day. Similarly, when Bethany tries to explain why her grandfather's bar mitzvah took place in Nuremburg, which was not his hometown, she says, "His bar mitzvah he had in Nuremburg, where he had family or friends or something." In Bethany's post-Holocaust world, a bar mitzvah is a time when family and friends are present to partake in the celebration. Of course, Bethany resembles nothing short of the entire post-Holocaust world in her inability to comprehend. That is, Bethany's interview reiterates Dori Laub's (Felman & Laub, 1992) notion of the Holocaust as an event without a witness. As Kaplan states, "Consequently, those who actually did witness the atrocities of the Holocaust are either dead or suffered too much to ever know what actually happened to them." (1996, p. 218). She goes on to explain, "Only the survivors can testify, and since (in order to survive) they could not be fully present during their own massive traumatization, even they cannot truly bear witness" (Kaplan, 1996, p. 218).

Tapping into the "hierarchy of suffering" (Bar-On, 1995) that has evolved regarding Holocaust experiences, Bethany discusses her grandmother's belief that she is not a Holocaust survivor, although she survived the Holocaust:

> My grandfather was in a concentration camp, so... I think that being married to someone [like that] she doesn't really consider herself a Holocaust survivor. And I remember her telling me something: they had gone to a synagogue where everybody is a Holocaust survivor where they're like all old Jewish people, and she said there was an event and they were honoring all the Holocaust survivors and they told all the Holocaust survivors to stand up and come up and like have a, I don't know, an *aliyah*, or something. And she didn't go up and she said, "I'm not a Holocaust survivor," and that really... I

was like, "But you are a Holocaust survivor." She went through hiding, her father got caught in the war, she… you know, she always talks about what she hates the most is that she never went to college and that she never got to go to high school, and she's not stupid but she never got… she stopped going to school when she was 10 years old or something. And she, you know, I think she's saying like she had jury duty and they cut her in the jury as someone who's not bright because she hasn't graduated high school, and she's like, "But I'm not like that." She was never allowed to graduate high school. So like things like that. She's definitely a Holocaust survivor. She's definitely a survivor. But she doesn't even consider herself one. And I think it's just because she didn't get tortured to death, or whatever.

Bethany's grandmother's insistence that she is not a Holocaust survivor likely stems from her sense that others suffered more deeply. Because she "didn't get tortured to death," she feels she cannot serve as a witness to this massive collective trauma. Along this line of thinking, there is no such thing as a witness, as anyone who did "get tortured to death" is no longer alive to provide a testimony. Indeed, Bethany's grandmother is not alone in this belief. In the same way that Bethany's generation will never comprehend the atrocity, and Bethany's grandmother cannot understand the experience of someone who went through a concentration camp, Bethany's grandfather will never know what it was like to die in a gas chamber, as his brother did. Thus, people's construction of hierarchies of suffering speaks to their feelings of alienation from, or closeness to, the event.

The Mechanism of Transmission

Numerous behavioral and emotional patterns emerged in Bethany's interview that linked her grandparents' generation, to her father's, to her own. The first example of this was in discussion of excessive guilt amongst her family members. Recognizing the debilitating impact of such guilt was relatively straightforward when exploring her father's lifestyle.

> My mom always says, "You know he's a Holocaust survivor child because he doesn't enjoy his life ever." That's probably her way of bashing my dad or something, but he doesn't like to go on vacation, he works really, really hard all the time… people always say he's not the normal Jewish doctor because he works so hard and he does everything around the house. Whereas most people hire people to do things, he fixes everything, he makes everything, he has to mow the lawn every week, and we don't ever have a gardener… all those kinds of things. And we always say they resort back to…. I think he probably feels guilty that his parents went through that so he can't enjoy every piece of life because they had to go through that… suffer.

Because Bethany's grandparents suffered through the Holocaust, likely plagued by guilt that they survived while so many others did not, their son unconsciously feels that he does not deserve to live his life to the fullest. He imposes superfluous methods to ensure that he does not "enjoy his life ever," thereby joining with his parents in their past suffering. Logically, of course, this does not make sense; her father's guilt and suffering will not undo her grandparents' experiences, nor will it lessen their pain. Kestenberg's (1972) term "transposition" captures the phenomenon by which a parent's past experiences overwhelm the child's present reality: the past occupies a vast amount of psychological space in the present, and the construct of time is reversed between parent and child. The child's existence unfolds within the parent's past (Kaplan, 1996).

Kaplan (1996) suggests that a child who senses her parent's unspoken shame, guilt and terror is inspired to recreate these circumstances in order to concretize and ultimately cure the parent's trauma. However, she does not address the possibility that a survivor's child might enact a comparable scenario without any insight into his or her actions or subsequent working through, leaving the pattern to be repeated and the work incomplete. Perhaps it is not the survivor's children who can fully testify as to what happened to their parents, but more so their grandchildren, who have the additional perspective of intergenerational dynamics following the traumatic event. Furthermore, while familial silence and secrecy can motivate a child's quest to uncover what happened to the parent, the weight of this journey may be too heavy for a child who witnessed his parents' traumatic symptoms first-hand. For all of these reasons, Bethany has been the first in her family to serve as her grandparents' and father's bridge to life. Her curiosity allows her to begin examining both her grandparents' and father's past trauma, and may lessen the need for future reenactments of past experiences.

Indeed, Bethany recognizes her own battles with guilt and effortlessly links this instinctive reaction to her grandparents' traumatic history and her fantasy that she might have saved them:

> Like, it wasn't what would my parents think, or what would mom say if I brought home a non-Jew, which is usually what most Jewish girls would say. But I was just thinking in my head, oh my God how could I do this to my grandparents? And it would make me feel so guilty because they are these old, nice people who had such terrible lives, and then I'm like how could I do this? So it's a lot of guilt... more than anything. And in my head, my grandparents are these old, they need help, they're so sweet, they're so nice... you just feel bad for your grandparents and then I feel like a hundred times worse, like oh my God what did they have to go through their whole lives, to think that my grandfather lost his entire family and he never had parents and I just feel so *bad* all the time. Anytime that comes into my head, I just want to start crying for him. But to me he's just this little old man that I just want to protect from anything, and I couldn't protect him from that.

Bethany's insight into her guilt surpasses her father's in that she verbalizes feeling "bad all the time" for her grandparents and wanting desperately to protect them from their past. Bethany's guilt therefore arises whenever she imagines they might disapprove of her decisions: "...they are these old, nice people who had such terrible lives and then I'm like how could I do this?" Thus, intergenerational lifestyle patterns in Bethany's family run the gamut from choice of food and romantic

CHAPTER THREE

partners to religious observances. Following a discussion about her grandfather being forced to eat a dead horse on the death march in Auschwitz, Bethany describes currently knowing her grandfather as a picky eater who "won't try new foods." She reveals, "And when he was finally liberated... I just found this out recently... he was liberated with pasta and he won't eat pasta anymore... he won't eat pizza either but that he says because of the smell, which is beyond me why he doesn't eat pizza." While my first association to Bethany's grandfather not eating pizza related to ovens and a constant smell of something burning, I put these thoughts aside at the time. However, minutes later in the interview, the conversation about ovens and deadness ensued:

> B: My grandmother makes everything. I don't even think he knows how to turn on the oven. Or the stove or anything.
> N: And is your dad a picky eater?
> B: Well he's a vegetarian and he doesn't eat a lot at all. And my mom says that he doesn't love food like a normal person loves food. He eats for necessity for living, not for pleasure. Whereas I definitely eat for pleasure (laughing) and like my brothers who eat tons.
> N: What's his reason for being a vegetarian?
> B: Animal reasons. (Silence.)
> N: How about you?
> B: I don't eat that much meat, I don't really like it...

Bethany's father eats for necessity, not for pleasure, ensuring that he himself could eat a dead horse if forced to. While Bethany does not explicitly verbalize these links between the generations, she leads the conversation in such a way that the transmission of historically-based behaviors and emotions is clear. At times, however, it seems that Bethany's family does not want to acknowledge these links:

> I was really shocked that I never knew that my grandfather's brother's name was Tommy until I started learning about it when I was older. And my first dog that I ever had we named Tommy. And when I found that out I was like, how could we have named our dog after our great-

> uncle who had meant so much to my grandfather? Like, what could he have thought? I was like, I feel so terrible. And we ended up giving him away after a couple years, but what did my grandfather think when we said, "We named our dog Tommy"? And I was distraught about this. Tommy had been gone for years, but it was like how could we have named a dog after my grandfather's brother? I was just so upset about it.

Whether Bethany's dog was named Tommy to help her father master feelings towards the name or as an expression of anger towards his father and his life circumstances is unclear. However, towards the end of the interview, Bethany found a way for me to experience her family's dynamic first-hand. About 75 minutes into the interview, Bethany remembered that she had promised to call her father at a certain time in order to be picked up from the interview. She had lost track of time, and called him later than he expected.

> B: [On the phone: Hi, sorry, I'm at Nirit's, I'm sorry… I'm sorry, I'm sorry, I didn't have my phone (laughing). I'm sorry, dad. It's right here but Nirit's been interviewing me so I couldn't answer it. I got here late, I got here late. I'm sorry. I thought you said it was fine. I told you I would be here for an hour but I didn't get here on time. I need like five to 10 more minutes here. I'll be down in five minutes. Sorry.] He thought I died. (Laughing). Oh God. Alright, sorry.
> N: Sorry about that. I didn't think of that.
> B: He's like, I thought you died. Okay.
> N: Did he say that?
> B: He Googled you and everything and he's like wandering the streets.
> N: Oh no…
> B: He was like, "I've been Googling Nirit Gradwohl." I just should have called him and said I may not be done…
> N: He's very protective of you.

As Bethany is in the midst of an interview about the intergenera-

CHAPTER THREE

tional transmission of Holocaust trauma, her father circles my block in expectation that Bethany will not come out alive. While fear and expectation of death are understandably common experiences for the children of survivors, there is a sense that the interview's subject matter is increasingly threatening. What might Bethany discover? Will it kill her? Will it destroy her family? Is it possible to talk and cry and feel without complete disintegration? Or must defenses be in place to protect us from the truth of a traumatic world?

In search of her place within a collective narrative, Bethany has begun the work in her family. She asks, she narrates, she comforts, and she heals. In a sense, Bethany recognizes that her life has been and will continue to be dedicated to her ancestors. She will find a way to work through their past traumas regardless of life circumstances:

> I know that whenever I had an opportunity to write a school paper or talk about someone important in my life—every class, every year—that's always what I wrote about. Like, I remember when we learned about pilgrims, I wrote about my grandmother... how she was a pilgrim and came to this country and that she grew up in France where there were pogroms every day. And when they asked "name someone who is your pilgrim," she was my pilgrim. And whenever I had to do "who is your hero," my grandfather was my hero. And "why is he your hero?" Because he was in concentration camp. And I never... not that I don't think that about my other grandparents, but I grew up until 12th grade I had all four grandparents and I never wrote about my other grandparents that way. I mean, maybe I did but I can't remember. But I specifically remember when we learned about pilgrims I wrote about my grandmother. For *every* project I've ever had has been about my grandparents I think...

Bethany turned her school projects into conversations about her Holocaust survivor grandparents. For every topic and for every project, Bethany found a link; this is because for Bethany, nothing else exists as long as Holocaust trauma does. She will write excessively, talk excessively, and cry excessively because she is strong enough to write, talk and cry. She has absorbed an entire history of suffering, and only by doing the work of mourning will she answer her ancestors' cry for help.

> N: And how is it now to talk about it?
> B: It's fine to talk about it because I talk about it a lot. I actually spoke to... I worked at a public school in Boston and their eighth grade was learning about the Holocaust so I spoke to every single eighth grade class and it's a huge public school and I told them our story. And all my friends know my grandparents... it's something that comes... that I talk about a lot. So, it's not hard to talk about it, but if I were to... I don't know, sometimes it makes me cry. Every eighth grade class I cried in. Every 25 minutes I was crying. Can't I stop crying already? I know this story, and I know what's gonna happen at the end. I was also really nervous and these kids never met a Jew before in their lives and they knew me and they didn't know I was Jewish.
> N: A lot of pressure.
> B: Yeah, I wanted to make sure I actually got the point across to them.
> N: As if saying it so many times would take the feeling away.
> B: Right, I thought it would, but... I was like, I wonder if I'm even going to cry before I went. And then I cried in every single period and I was like oh my God. And I spoke at my synagogue once and I cried there... and I was like, I need to stop crying.

Bethany has dedicated her life to curing her ancestors' Holocaust trauma. She has moved past the phase of acting out situations of guilt, shame, and terror in order to concretize and engage the unfathomable; instead, she allows herself to wallow in their past suffering, thereby mourning the loss and pain that her grandparents and father needed desperately to suppress. In working through her family's collective trauma, the present can exist in its own right, the family can begin to heal, and new narrative possibilities can start to emerge.

CHAPTER 4: LEAH

> I'm extremely obsessive-compulsive, not the type of person that diagnoses themselves. Like, in high school, I was seeing somebody for it. I schedule everything and plan everything, so whenever something goes off course, big or small, I have real difficulty dealing with it and that tends to make me feel guilty. And I don't know when I developed that OCD or where that came from. Potentially that's related...

Leah, a 23-year-old, third generation Holocaust descendant, tenuously links her personality and lifestyle to her history as the granddaughter of survivors. "Potentially that's related" she half states and half wonders, having just revealed this personal information three quarters of the way into her hour and a half interview on the topic of intergenerational transmission of trauma. Her insight arrives on the heels of her maternal grandparents' story:

> I know that my grandparents... they had a five-year-old son and he was shot on the street by a Nazi soldier in front of my grandmother. My mom wasn't born yet... this would've been my mom's brother... my mom wasn't born, she never met him... so he was killed when he was five and my grandparents were both taken... they were already married and had a family... they were both taken to Auschwitz, separated, lost each other, and ended up finding each other afterwards.

In the context of her ancestral trauma, Leah's obsessive-compulsive tendencies may serve a number of protective functions: first, she preserves a sense of control in her life by mentally planning every hour of the day, having learned early on that the world is unpredictable and painful. Second, she struggles to master a part of her traumatic history, in that order might undo her family's tragic loss. Along these lines, she unconsciously imagines that by deliberately inspecting every hour of the day, nothing could feel out of control and no one could catch her off guard; thus, her grandparents' son might be saved. Third, Leah engages in thinking to avoid feeling. Perhaps her mind is absorbed by thoughts and lists such that little time or space remains for the emotional burden of past traumas. Finally, Leah's obsessive-compulsive symptoms provide an observable entity, which she can pinpoint as the cause of her pain. Cyrulnik (2005) describes how a person feels relief when she can finally name the source of her inner suffering: "I can join a group and express what I'm feeling. I can consult a doctor and show him a symptom. I'm no longer alone in the world. I now know what I have to deal with and how to get help from people close to me and from my culture" (p. 101).

Leah herself echoes this sentiment: "I just needed somebody to say, like, 'Oh, you have an actual thing with a name, you can blame that, you don't have to blame yourself...'" However, underneath this assertion, like other third generation survivors, Leah does to some extent blame herself: "...whenever something goes off course, big or small, I have real difficulty dealing with it and that tends to make me feel guilty," she says in the opening quote. Indeed, something "big," or more accurately, of massive proportions, has gone "off course." Until her family's trauma is confronted and, as Leah says, "dealt with," she will continue to exist within the shadows of a ghost.

Secrets…

Leah begins her interview by stating, "I actually don't know that much about my father's side of the family. Both of his parents were Holocaust survivors." She explains the absence of knowledge with, "We always just sort of went to my mom's side of the family. We were closer with them anyway and they were more open, and as I'll explain, they have a much more obvious link." She adds, "Even my dad, from what he knows, isn't that good at remembering it or sharing it or as deeply impacted as my mom. She talks about it." The "much more obvious link" Leah is referring to is the ghost of a murdered child who is present every day in the life of this family. In contrast, Leah's father and paternal grandparents were not as "open" and, in Leah's mind, not "as deeply impacted" by their Holocaust experiences. As opposed to her mother, they did not "talk about it." We are left to wonder about Leah's paternal side of the family, who was likely debilitated by internal anguish and unable to give voice to unfathomable experiences. As Judith Herman writes, "The conflict between the will to deny horrible events and the will to proclaim them aloud is the central dialectic of psychological trauma ... But far too often secrecy prevails, and the story of the traumatic event surfaces not as a verbal narrative but as a symptom" (1997, p. 1).

Indeed, the denial of suffering and devastating silences mold a family's way of life, implicitly deemed the only tolerable way of life, and transmitted from generation to generation. When asked about her father's father, Leah recalls:

> He was a very quiet man... he was a very nice man, he absolutely wasn't bitter at all, he was just quiet. He would sit in the chair, we would go to school and come home and he would just be sitting in his chair. He made his own meals. He didn't need anybody to make them for him. He just did his own thing. Even like, he passed away in his sleep, very quietly. You know, he was just this quiet old man.

Leah's assertion that her grandfather "absolutely wasn't bitter at all" and was just "a quiet old man" hints at the possibility of his emotional numbing. Perhaps he did not "need" anything or anyone because he found safety in his isolation from the world, going through the motions of life without any real contact or connection. Likewise, Leah has learned to take what she sees at face value, accepting the dynamics at play: "...he would just be sitting in his chair." Similarly, in speaking about her relationship with her father, Leah states, "I know much less about him. He's just a more introverted person. But that's the sort of relationship we have; when we're together, we're not speaking about world issues or my life, we're just making fun of people that walk by." Leah's descriptions of her father and father's father are matter-of-fact, encouraging the interviewer not to overstep the surface-level descriptions Leah's family has long upheld. Furthermore, her tone indirectly expresses: this is the way it is; there is no need to question myself or my beliefs. Unfortunately, these boundaries reiterate the family's primary struggle, for denial ultimately fortifies trauma. As the subtitle of Davoine and Gaudillière's (2004) book suggests, *Whereof One Cannot*

Speak, Thereof One Cannot Stay Silent.

Alongside silence and secrecy, symptoms persist throughout the generations. Of her father's sister, who lived with her survivor parents until their death, Leah says:

> Oh, I mean like crazy... she hadn't been taking her medications; she had been eating all the wrong things. Like, there was old food thrown around the house. It reeked when my parents first got there. They found something like over $20 in change just in one day strewn about the house. She had bags and bags of, for instance, leather gloves that she had bought, never opened, never worn. She had an entire bag of different pairs of silver earrings... As if you were going out and you wanted a pair of silver hoop earrings so you bought every one you could find and figured you could decide later and return them, and she just never returned them. She never cleaned out the house from her parents' stuff, but after my grandfather passed away she moved out of her bedroom into what was their master bedroom, but she so cluttered her own bedroom that they couldn't even open the door. She would go on like business trips and she wouldn't unpack her suitcase when she came home, so she just went and bought another suitcase and packed it with new clothes. She had dozens of packed suitcases with the tags still on them so my parents could tell where she'd been and where she'd gone.

Clearly, this daughter of Holocaust survivors spent a lifetime mired in the internal devastation of her parents' experience. Never having found a place within language, her family's unmourned suffering flooded her post-Holocaust life. One can only fantasize about the significance of silver hoop earrings and leather gloves; do such accessories represent fragments of knowledge in an existence that unfolds outside of language? What of the numerous packed suitcases, which suggest a preparedness to flee yet an inability to truly escape one's baggage? "...she just never returned them," Leah says of the earrings, speaking volumes about her aunt's incapacity to "return" and rework the original trauma. As Cyrulnik writes,

> This is how emotional restriction constitutes a major sensory privation, an insidious trauma that is all the more damaging because it's hard to become aware of it, to make it into an event, a memory that we could confront and rework. When we don't come face-to-face with a recollection, it haunts us, like a shadow in our inner world, and instead of working on it, it works on us (2005, p. 6).

Consequently, while from Leah's point of view we have not yet broached the noteworthy aspects of her family history, it is impossible to escape the power of a secret, "working... on us."

...Ghosts...

N: I'm really interested in going back to your grandparents' son who was killed. Do you know what his name was?
L: Robert.
N: Robert. Did his name get reused later?
L: My middle name is Rosie; that comes from him. And they had a portrait of him in my grandparents' bedroom... I only saw one apartment, but before I was born they had a few and they always had this picture of him and you can tell—it looks exactly like my brother. My whole family looks alike, like a lot alike. It was my grandfather transferring right into my brother. You can see my mom's face in there; you can see me in there.
N: Wow, what was that like?
L: You know, as much as I have heard about it and I feel like... Not that I understand their experience, but that I'm familiar with their experience... I can't ever imagine it. You know, it's such a horrible loss to not even really get to bury your child because of the circumstances. And I think that their fear of ever losing my mom was so le-

gitimate even though it drove her crazy. You know, he's just this kid that I never met, that I never could have... I definitely can't even imagine as an older child or a man because my mom didn't have any other brothers. There's not like there's somebody that you can see him as. I have no idea what he is to me except that he's just this face in this picture.

N: Right, a face with whom you share similarities. I mean, physically, anyway.

L: Right, like, you can see my brother in there. I mean, I can't think of it as if it was my brother. I can't even imagine that horrible loss. At this point I've lost all of my grandparents so I've experienced death, but not the way you would losing your baby like that.

Leah and her family exist within the subsistence of a five-year-old ghost. In every picture, every mirror, every conversation with her brother, every interaction with a child, and perhaps every encountered "face," hers and that of an "other," the ghost is present. The concrete, visual similarity makes this ghost entirely unavoidable: "It was my grandfather transferring right into my brother. You can see my mom's face in there; you can see me in there." The "much more obvious link" Leah spoke about previously is better understood with this context—what cannot be spoken in this family is tangible and all-consuming, a truth that resurfaces and repeats itself through time. In his *Specters of Marx* (1994), Derrida maintains that a person's life is shaped by attempts to give voice to inner ghosts. He writes:

> Repetition and first time: this is perhaps the question of the event as question of the ghost .... Repetition and first time, but also repetition and last time, since the singularity of any first time makes of it also a last time. Each time it is the event itself, a first time is a last time. Altogether other. Staging for the end of history. Let us call it a hauntology (Derrida, 1994, p. 10).

"Each time it is the event itself," as the haunted and the haunting become one and the same. Leah states, "He's just this kid that I never met," as though "this kid" is an existing person in present time, waiting to be found. Indeed, he is real; alive within her and directing the course of her life.

The metaphor of the "portrait" of a ghost is a powerful one. Derrida's specter, or revenant, invisibly occupies a space that vaguely exists somewhere between the "occupied" and the "occupier" (1994, p. 172). Leah states, "Right, like, you can see my brother in there. I mean, I can't think of it as if it was my brother. I can't even imagine that horrible loss. At this point I've lost all of my grandparents so I've experienced death, but not the way you would losing your baby like that." From brother to baby and baby to brother, the past engulfs the present and the present is the past. "...a first time is a last time. Altogether other," Derrida writes. Thus, the portrait of a ghost manifests both visible and invisible truths, forever a foreign occupier which Leah cannot grasp. She says, "There's not like there's somebody that you can see him as." In other words, he is me but he is not me, he is everything but he is nothing. "I have no idea what he is to me..." she concludes; after all, how well can you really know a ghost?

Within her daily life, and stories about her daily life, the ghost repeatedly shows his face. For example, Leah describes frequent arguments with her mother: "Like, I'll snap at her and she will... I don't want to say she goes off because she doesn't yell, but she gives the cold shoulder like a *five-year-old* might. And it's something I've inherited. So then she and I end up in this cold war..." How does a five-year-old give a cold shoulder? Instantaneously, Leah and her mother are transformed, back into the world of a slaughtered five-year-old brother. Leah's mother turns a "cold shoulder" away from her daughter in the presence of this ghost, and the world turns cold. "So then she and I end up in this cold war," Leah speaks, right back in the original setting, as each time "it is the event itself." Leah continues to show the ways in which the dead remain a part of life:

> N: How do you think it impacted your mom that her parents' first child was a boy and their second child was a girl?
> L: What do you mean?
> N: Any sense of loss of a man?
> L: In terms of loss of a man, I don't think so at all. My

mom and my grandfather were very close, they used to sit and read the newspaper together and watch TV together, so any of those things were like a father wants his son to do those things. I never got the sense that he felt he missed out on any of that. My grandfather *adored* my brother and he would follow him anywhere and whatever my brother said was wonderful, and my grandmother did with me, which is interesting because in my family it's kind of the opposite. I think we were just the idealized versions of what they didn't think they had. Like, I never thought of my grandmother the way she probably feels my mom did, but at the same time she never understood that me and my mom had a similar relationship to what she had. So I think for them it probably spooked them out that my brother looked so much like this kid and maybe that's what made the connection there really strong. But I don't think it's something they would have ever... how can you say someone reminds you of someone that's dead? It's not something like... six of us sit down at the table and say, "Hey, everyone realizes they looked alike, right?"

N: They might not have even realized it...

L: Yeah, but it's like something where my mom and I commented on it, my brother commented on it. It's that obvious.

N: So the two of you were like the idealized siblings, like the two kids they could've had...

L: Yeah, I mean, they, you know, we were their only grandchildren. They fawned over us. We were decent kids—we didn't give our parents any trouble, we get along very well... my grandmother always had this real romantic notion that he would end up marrying one of my friends and I would end up marrying one of his friends because we're so close in age. That's something actually I needed to mention: my mom so much hated being an only child that she had my brother and immediately got pregnant with me, obviously, because she just wanted to start trying immediately so that he would have a sibling, and then she wanted to keep going but my dad was like, "We have two babies, chill." Sort of like the only-child syndrome.

What I fail to realize in my questioning of Leah, but what she quickly reminds me, is that sex and gender are insignificant in the memorialization of her dead. Her mother was created to reinstate her lost brother, and to do all the things "a father wants his son to do." After all, as Kaplan (1996) explains, survivor parents who have lost family members in the Holocaust consciously wish that their post-Holocaust family will replace the family members that were killed; the parent's unconscious wish, however, is that each new child will serve as the return of a dead one. Leah's mother, therefore, was to complete her brother's prematurely interrupted life prior to carrying out her own. We cannot know to what extent she lived a life in her own right; however, Leah clearly states, "My mom so much hated being an only child that she had my brother and immediately got pregnant with me, obviously, because she just wanted to start trying immediately so that he would have a sibling..." The weight of not having had a sibling was intense, one that her mother was unwilling to repeat for her children. While Leah suggests that her father convinced her mother to "chill" and stop after "two babies," Leah and her brother have in turn been created as the two siblings who might undo the family's past trauma. Leah states, "I think we were just the idealized versions of what they didn't think they had." Indeed, not having two children, a son along with a daughter, was ever-present.

"My mom and my grandfather were very close, they used to sit and read the newspaper together and watch TV together, so any of those things were like a father wants his son to do those things. I never got the sense that he felt he missed out on any of that." Again, a protective screen is in place that limits Leah from fully seeing what she already knows. Because she was not her brother, Leah's mother could never be enough. "My grandfather *adored* my brother" Leah says, though he was "spooked" by the reemergence of his murdered son a generation later. Perhaps, then, my heightened awareness of Leah's mother as a woman, and of Leah as a woman, was related to a sense of gender splitting in this family. "...whatever my brother said was wonderful, and my grandmother did with me, which is interesting because in my family it's kind of the opposite." Earlier in the interview, a similar gender divide arose:

> I was in my freshman year of college when my grandmother died and I saw it rip apart my mom and I think a lot of that was that she felt guilty for the way that she had treated her. So what my mom did was… she wasn't necessarily protective of me… she and I also used to butt heads a bunch… there was a stubborn streak. I was always like a daddy's girl and my brother was really close with my mom more so than my father. And she always tried to knock it into me that I had to respect her more.

During the interview, I was left feeling unclear about the details: Who is close with whom? Which child resembles which parent? Why does that matter? What is the significance of this sense of preference for one parent, or one child? Perhaps these gender splits represent the various fragments within each person, or the more general fragmentation of life during and since the Holocaust. Or maybe these questions relate to the shame, pride, and envy associated with Leah's knowledge that she is not a boy, and therefore not like the lost boy so memorialized in her family.

In response to my question about any recent dreams or nightmares, Leah says:

> L: Nothing really specific. I mean, I've had nightmares about losing people in our family. But they were never specific, like I don't want to go near water because I had a dream where my mom drowned. Nothing like that.
> N: But it was usually about one of your parents?
> L: Usually my brother, actually. You know, we're very close. I think a part of me always felt like that would be the hardest person.

The terror of losing her brother overwhelms her dreams. He is both the special child that the family values and remains worried about, but also unenviable in his constant closeness to death. Having been born a girl, Leah both loses and wins.

CHAPTER FOUR

...And Surrounding Shadows

In explaining how her sense of guilt is related to her obsessive-compulsive tendencies, Leah describes having "dragged out" her brother Friday night, only to result in his losing his coat. "It's not a tragedy," she says, "but I feel horrible about it... I get in my head this is the way things are going to go. I expect everything to be perfect." Similarly, she reveals her need to continuously check certain items and create detailed lists that organize every hour of the day:

> L: I'll go back and check things. I have certain routines. Not in like my apartment now, but my bedroom in New Hampshire, the door has to be closed a certain way. I'll schedule—get ready with the same routine every morning.
> N: Like, shower and then do something?
> L: Yeah, even like put in the mouthwash, while the mouthwash is in, go back to my room and like take out my hair gel, take off the cap, then go back and spit out the mouthwash, then go put in your hair gel... things like that. You know, if my roommate gets up and goes in the bathroom when I need to go back, I'll be like... ugh.
> N: You'll walk yourself through like little things...
> L: Yeah, it's always been manageable, it's not like a crazy thing, but it's a little weird...

Indeed, losing a coat is not a tragedy. Yet, being out of control has led to tragedy in her family history. While Leah worries that her habits might be perceived as crazy, she also reveals a sense of ownership over her compulsions. After my asking whether her brother shares any of these tendencies, Leah responds, "My parents think he's a little compulsive also, but I just think he's bossy." In a sense, Leah insinuates that this is hers and hers is different. Consciously, however, Leah takes herself out of the competition: "I don't feel upstaged nor do I feel the need to upstage someone else and I don't understand why other people do." She is an actress in an old script, constantly upstaged, but long since taken herself out of the running for lead role.

Leah goes on to describe how her grandfather similarly "stuck to his routine." She says, "And my mother always attributed that to his experience where they were just so shell-shocked that they just clung to this routine of normalcy that they created for themselves afterwards. Very old fashioned in that sense." While she does not directly link the "routine of normalcy" to her own life, she indirectly reveals how her daily routine reflects a "shell-shocked" reaction to intergenerationally transmitted experiences. For example, she says, "I fully admit I have no street smarts… oh, I get lost everywhere. If I get myself into some situation, I'm just not smart enough to get myself out of it. You know, I can ride the train all around the city before I figure out where to get off." Understandably, Leah has "no street smarts," because one cannot have street smarts in a world that allows a five-year-old to be shot on the streets. In these ways, she continues to live within the shadow of the Holocaust in a post-Holocaust world.

Nevertheless, Leah's strength and hope persevere. In thinking about her family's suffering, she also reminds herself:

> It seems to me that the thing that I always found most beautiful is that they found each other again. That they clearly instilled in my mother, their only child, a real sense of Judaism. I think of it as like, I know all I need to know to be really proud of them, and to be happy for them, even though it's been hard for them… to think that they succeeded in coming out of it.

While Leah has not come "out of it," she finds herself partaking in an interview, honestly discussing her family history, and entertaining new and conflicting ideas. Exhibiting great courage and resilience, she allows herself to exist fully "inside of it." Similarly, in reflecting on what she might want to do differently as a mother, Leah says:

> My brother and I have always talked about how we want to keep our families close with one another. We didn't have any cousins because my dad had this crazy sister, my mom was an only child, so we're really looking forward to being able to give our kids cousins, which is something that we always talked about. Other than that, I imagine, I'm a lot like my mom who is a lot like her mom, so I imagine I'll be a lot like that.

CHAPTER FOUR

Like her own mother, Leah wishes to expand the size of her family, thereby welcoming additional players that might bring fresh insight and support. As Leah continues to "butt heads" with history and allows herself to remain fully in it—examining pride but also shame, happiness but also sadness—she evolves from an actress in an old script to a part of something altogether original.

CHAPTER 5: YAEL

> N: Did you ever feel there was anything about your family history that you didn't know... like a feeling that a piece was missing?
> Y: No.
> N: That's amazing.
> Y: My family was very open.

As I sat with 23-year-old Yael, a half-Israeli, half-American, third generation Holocaust descendant, I considered her proclamation that secrets and silences were not a part of her family's experience. How *amazing*, I remarked, struck by the simultaneous presence and absence of the unknown in our conversation. Re-reading my personal reaction to Yael's interview, I recall feeling both intrigued and thwarted by elements of the "unsayable" (Rogers, 2006) in Yael's narrative. "No ... My family was very open." Josette Garon (2004), translating and quoting Pontalis (2002) on the motivation for becoming a therapist, states, "'Where do you live? In the vicinity of the unknown'; 'what do you do? I try to guess the presence of secrets'" (p. 85). In contrast to the silence so pervasive in other families of Holocaust survivors, here I encountered a family who valued speeches, founded memorials, and emphasized the communication of their grandfather's story. Nevertheless, I was left wondering about the unknown, or unspoken, elements of Yael's experience. Yael begins:

> Growing up, my grandfather was very vocal. He helped establish various Holocaust museums and always went to go speak, and from a very young age I knew his story, whereas his brother took his name off his arm and never spoke about it. So it's very weird seeing me and my first cousins as opposed to my grandfather's brother's grandchildren... just very different upbringings on knowing about the Holocaust. My grandfather did everything... he survived Birkenau which is the death camp of Aus-

chwitz. He did the death march with his father. He's been to numerous death camps and was very... he was a big speaker and everywhere he went he was never afraid to tell kids, no matter how young they were, what happened and the horrors... he never shed that... he never kept that from us.

What is the nature of the unsayable in a family that is "very vocal" about past traumas? Does it persevere underneath the mask of language, or is it exhumed, deciphered, and even understood? In her opening statements alone, Yael addresses the dichotomy between knowing versus not knowing, speaking versus not speaking, and "shedding" versus "keeping" a memory. As we see in her slip, divergent qualities are distinguished from one another while remaining linked in a mutually defining relationship: "...he never shed that... he never kept that from us." Indeed, he could never "shed" his experiences, but rather "kept" his memories alive, consciously transferring them to his children and grandchildren. Interestingly, synonyms for the signifier "to keep from" include "protect," "shield," "shelter," "save," and "cushion." In transmitting his narrative to his offspring, Yael's grandfather did not protect them from the horrific truths of his experience. Thus, she grew up knowing, in great detail, her family history, and living within its context. At such a point, as Cyrulnik explains, "It is not a question of normal development, since the trauma inscribed in memory is part of the person's history from now on, like a ghost that accompanies him" (2005, p. 2).

Yet, despite a lifetime of "speaking" about the Holocaust, Yael exists within a narrative that she is unable to convey using language. "My grandfather did everything," she says, utilizing the verb "do," a neutral, active word suggesting a conscious decision on her grandfather's part. Furthermore, she states, he experienced "everything." While clearly her grandfather did not undergo "everything," it is impossible to convey to an audience what it means to survive Birkenau, the death march, and numerous other death camps. For her grandfather and an entire population of Holocaust survivors and descendants living after the event itself, nothing and no one can capture this massive trauma, regardless of consistent efforts to impart the experience. He "did everything," and yet we understand nothing of the events. In contrast, remaining silent is associated with a loss of identity: "his brother took his name off his arm and never spoke about it." That is, her grandfather's brother removed the number tattooed on his arm at Auschwitz, "never spoke about it," and, in a sense, removed his name.

Yael proudly states, "...he was never afraid to tell kids, no matter how young they were, what happened and the horrors..." One cannot help but wonder: What is the impact of knowing "the horrors" at such a young age? How do children learn to contain and incorporate historical knowledge into their identities? To what extent are self-blame, guilt, fear, and shame transmitted, leaving these children burdened by the pain and suffering of an entire people? Yael honestly reveals:

> Y: There's a recurring nightmare that I actually still have… I'll have it like once a year, twice a year; it's in my house in Philadelphia growing up. It's just the only dream that I have that's recurring and I'm walking, well not walking… you know the British, the redcoat army? They're like marching after me and I'm running away from them and I always hide in the same bush… and that's the only part of the dream I remember. But I always tell people and they think it's because of the Nazis… because they would just be like, who has an image of like an army marching after you?
> N: And it's just you?
> Y: Yeah, it's just me like running away and I always hide in this bush in front of my house but that's the only part of the dream that I remember when I wake up.
> N: What do you make of it?
> Y: What do you mean?
> N: Well, you said other people related it to the Nazis. Do you think it's connected?
> Y: Probably, (laughing) because the dreams probably started young and I heard some pretty horrible stories when I was young… I don't know if I had nightmares when I was younger but I know that's one nightmare that has always been recurring and it's really scary.

In responding to my question of how old she was when she began hearing her grandfather's stories, Yael stated, "Never a time when I haven't been. I'm sure at some point they started telling it to me, but I don't know an age where they sat me down and were like 'We're going to teach you about the Holocaust.' It was always who we were." Her recurring nightmare is an example of a concrete entrance of her grandfather's history into her present-day experience; after all, the nightmare is now hers. Furthermore, as Davoine and Gaudillière (2004) explain:

> In general, when the world becomes nonsense, children tend to think that they are the cause of the catastrophe, since this is the only way they can make sense of it to themselves ... it is better to assume that one is oneself the cause of an inexplicable event, or to unload it onto the other, than to confront an event without a reason. This is one of the most effective survival strategies in the face of the uncanny, the strange and disturbing field of the Real (p. 72).

Believing that she is, somehow, the source of the catastrophe, Yael undertakes a mission to "avenge" her grandfather for the crimes committed against him. Therefore, the Holocaust becomes not merely a part of Yael's collective and individual identity, but the basic infrastructure through which her world is shaped. What Garon (2004, p. 88) calls a trans-generational "alien transplant" takes root, infiltrating her conscious and unconscious life.

Past Becomes Present...

Yael's sense of ownership regarding her grandfather's pain can be seen in her hierarchical assignment of what survivors "went through":

> Y: And this is gonna sound horrible but it's fine... I never have seen *Schindler's List* or read Holocaust books or watched Holocaust movies... I just can't... not because I think it's horrible, but because I just never... I can't sympathize with other people's stories just because my grandfather's is so horrible. It reminds me of my grandfather and what my grandfather went through. When I hear other people's stories I'm like, "That's nothing

compared to what my grandfather went through." It just angers me that here they are speaking about their stories because it's not even close to, or like what I think is not as close to, what my grandfather went through, and it's just very hard for me to listen to anyone else's story besides my grandfather's.
N: Because in a way it feels like he suffered more...?
Y: Right, it's really ridiculous... I'm always resentful and think that my grandfather had it really, really horribly and went through a lot and... I know other people did too... but, like, when I hear people tell stories, like they hid in a forest and then were okay afterwards... it's really hard for me to come to terms with like... that's almost like cheating for me... so I tend to not...

In the above segment, Yael taps into a frequently mentioned sense of hierarchy regarding the degree to which a person "suffered" through and "survived" the Holocaust. The construction of such hierarchies reflects people's sense of disconnection from, or closeness to, the event. Interestingly, Yael is a third generation descendant of a survivor who maintains a powerful sense of ownership and protectiveness regarding her grandfather's pain. "I can't sympathize with other people's stories just because my grandfather's is so horrible," she says. In a sense, Yael feels that others do not know suffering the way her grandfather does. It seems that Yael has developed a sense of pride through the image of her grandfather as a unique survivor, not one of many but rather different and special. Perhaps she feels this distinctiveness reflects onto the remainder of her family. On a deeper level, however, it sounds as though she is actually describing a personal issue: "It just angers me that here they are speaking about their stories..." Why is she angered by other people's need and desire to speak? Perhaps this anger relates to a sense of envy that they have a story separate from her grandfather's. After all, Yael has spent her lifetime struggling to learn, remember, wrestle with, communicate, and further transmit her family history—an exhausting, all-consuming role. "But, like, when I hear people tell stories, like they hid in a forest and then were okay afterwards... it's really hard for me to come to terms with like... that's almost like cheating for me..." Certainly, a person who hides in a forest for months or years during war does not simply come out "okay afterwards." Her view of such people's experience as dishonest or dishonorable may be a projection of her own sense of guilt: she will always feel like she "cheated" in that she was born generations after the Holocaust and sidestepped the direct experience altogether. Her sense of responsibility for undoing her grandfather's past trauma is immense.

For various reasons, Yael winds up functioning within extremes: her grandfather is described as having experienced "everything," because otherwise he experienced nothing; he had to have suffered most, otherwise he did not suffer at all. Similarly, Yael connects such black and white thinking to her mother's outlook on the world:

> Y: She always brings up my grandfather ... Whenever I'm upset she's like, "You know, if your grandfather could hear you now... it's embarrassing, what would he say?" Like, because he was such a fighter and so strong and built himself up and like didn't give up that that's always my mom's way of... you know, she's always like, "You know what your grandfather went through, how can you be upset about something so trivial?"
> N: Like, "Get over it"?
> Y: Yeah, it's like not that big of a deal, if your grandfather can get over losing his whole family, like, you can get over this.
> N: That sounds so frustrating.
> Y: Yeah, like I'm still upset. I understand it's not that big of a deal, but still upset.

Here we see a short-circuiting of Yael's experience in the face of her family history, as her mother indicates that Yael does not deserve to experience the world in her own right following the historical trauma. Resonating with Yael's view that no one "went through" what her grandfather went through, her mother implies that because others suffered more deeply, Yael's harboring her own sense of loss or disappointment is superfluous. Yael is therefore left wondering: how dare I feel sadness (or fear or anger) unless I am starving, nearing death, and watching my family's murder in a concentration camp? Understandably, she feels "resentful" of other survivors' stories because on some level, she believes no one deserves a story aside from her grandfather—not she, not her mother, not anyone—not even her grandfather's brother who died before the Holocaust:

> My grandfather was 15 when the war started and he actually survived with his father but his father died the day of liberation from typhus, or typhoid, or something with a "typh"... and he lost a sister and his parents in the Holocaust. He also lost a brother but that was pre-Holocaust so it doesn't count.

For Yael, no one else counts the way her grandfather counts. In describing one of her grandfather's experiences in Auschwitz, she further reveals:

> And that's how he survived... in Birkenau, which was the death camp of Auschwitz... they needed a couple people there to take the wheelbarrow from the gas chambers to the crematorium. And so there would be a wheelbarrow where there would be two people in front and two people in back. My grandfather, the first time he did it, he was in the back... and the people in the front were shot... and he realized it was because... sorry, reverse. He was in the front and the people in the back got shot... and he realized that the Nazis were very smart and meticulous and wanted to get things done fast and if they killed the guys in the front it would take time to roll the wheelbarrow over their bodies, whereas if they killed the people in the back they could just keep going. So my grandfather always made sure he was the person in the front, and that was how he survived at Birkenau for a couple of weeks: being the guy in the front...

In order to survive, Yael's grandfather knew he had to be "the guy in the front." His strength and resourcefulness allowed her grandfather to survive even the death camp of Auschwitz. Furthermore, her grandfather not only survived, but built himself up and became what Yael calls, "the main guy in our whole entire family." Thus, "being the guy in the

CHAPTER FIVE

front" was a way of life for him, a necessary way of life for survival to be possible. With their grandfather in the front, Yael and her mother took up positions at "the back" of the wheelbarrow, serving as a buttress or support. Yael recalls, "My mom is—I think because of my grandfather—is like the most neurotic and anal woman you will ever meet in your whole life, like doesn't step away from my grandparents at all, like keeps them close all the time." Supporting her parents seems to have become her mother's full-time assignment.

As Yael reveals, her mother's "over-protectiveness" of her parents became characteristic of the family relationships in general:

> Y: Yeah, I know most people say they have overprotective mothers… mine's to a max, to an extreme. I think I talk to my mom six or seven times a day, minimum. If I'm out I'll be on the phone with my mom, tell her what I had for lunch, literally call my grandma and literally in that time my grandma will be like how was that sandwich? That's how often my family members talk. My mom… I remember Halloween when I was 13… you know when you're old enough to walk around by yourself? Like your Jewish neighborhood? My grandfather would be following me around in the car and my mom was hiding in bushes following me and my friends. They would really be over and beyond. It's remarkable how protective my mom is of everyone in her family, and it's not in a healthy way. People recognize that it's not in a healthy way but she, since my grandfather passed away, I don't know if she's left my grandma's side.
>
> N: Do you feel this gets in the way, or is it endearing and something you guys laugh about?
>
> Y: No, it gets in the way. Like, the type of thing where I know if I don't call her back in a couple hours easily there can be cops outside the apartment looking for me. It's happened. Like, my grandparents lived like a block away, and once when I was 15, we got a new puppy and I went to show my grandparents the new puppy and they weren't home… so I went next door and was there probably for 15 minutes and came out and there were

three cop cars because she didn't know where I was. So she's very neurotic... like, my parents split up and I think it's because she became increasingly more neurotic and more anal about every little thing. I don't know where it stems from...

Yael's family lives with a constant fear that a family member might be taken, killed, or suddenly go missing; these were the circumstances for Jews in Nazi Europe, where each day was potentially a person's last. Therefore, although Yael concludes her thoughts by saying, "I don't know where it stems from," suggesting a desire not to know, she does, of course, on some level know. Her knowledge allows her to link her mother's constant fear and anxiety both to her grandparents' experiences and to patterns in Yael's behavior:

It's very hard for me, the idea to leave my grandma and also my mom... like, my brother is going away, also abroad, and if all three of her kids are out of the country I don't know what she would do with herself—like I really don't. And I couldn't do that to her. There's so many things... like, I know if I see a phone call from her if I'm in the middle of class I have to call her back because she'll just go nuts. She just gets very panicky and like she always says she has an ulcer from worrying about us, but I don't feel bad about that because she brings it on herself the way she worries, and I hope that I'm not going to be like that. But I know with my grandmother, like... I can't tell you how many times when I'm home in Vermont, I call and I know she's home and I call her house and she doesn't answer... like, I'm driving—I immediately get in the car and start driving to her house which is now 20 minutes away. My mom finally moved 20 minutes away which is a huge guilt for my mom but I'll start driving there because, like, I don't know why she didn't answer her phone. Like, most of the time she's taking her dogs outside for a walk but, you know, me and my mom will stay in the same wavelength; one of us will be like, "Okay, we're on our way." It's just, so yeah...

> I guess I'm overprotective of my grandma but like not with my mom.

"I hope that I'm not going to be like that," Yael reflects before instantaneously detailing the ways in which she is, in fact, "like that." Her candid narrative reveals the paradoxical dynamic at play. Regardless of a conscious desire to break away from this arrangement, unconsciously she struggles to separate and individuate, as such growth might signify a rejection of her family. Concretely, as well, Yael's lifestyle choices are made "in the name of" her grandfather; for example, she says, "I always did the traditions for my grandfather to make him happy." Furthermore, as she possesses her own fears of abandonment and isolation, Yael finds herself simultaneously seeking safety within her family's enmeshment. A breakup with a boyfriend, safer than a breakup with her family, ultimately brings her into therapy. Thus, the cycle is reiterated and a middle ground is hard to come by; separation and individuation become dangerous developments, ones that could potentially cause someone to "go nuts":

> My brother is in Israel this year. It was a huge deal for my family and my mom letting him go. My brother just wasn't ready for college, like wasn't. He had to take a year off because he was failing high school—he would fail out of college—he needed a break. But it's been very, like my mom, I was in the car with my mom yesterday and my brother is coming home for a week next week and she was just like... literally, this is what she said: "Okay, don't forget, from the 14th to the 23rd, Michael's going to be home." She's like laying out every day and then said (crying voice), "And then January 2nd we're gonna take him back to the airport..." and then she started crying. Like, crying already about taking him back to the airport. That's just ridiculous. Whenever she thinks of him leaving, she cries like every day.

...And Present Becomes Past
Throughout most of her interview, Yael idealizes her grandfather in

the present tense; in her sporadic use of the past tense, she seems to suddenly remind herself that he is no longer alive. For example, Yael states, "He has no college education but he's smarter than any human." This present-tense description of her grandfather suggests that he is super-human, still alive and "smarter than" anyone. When she reveals a "rough," angry, and more vulnerable part of his personality, she quickly transforms her comment in an attempt to soften it, seeking to eliminate the possibility that anyone might view him as less than perfect:

> He was kind of the main guy in our whole entire family... like, I stayed at my grandparents' for three or four nights a week; they just, they were my parents. He was kind of a no-nonsense, no-bullshit grandfather; you know, very rough around the edges. He would yell. He played cards every night with his friends... he would yell and scream but everyone loved him for it.

In keeping with the family's tendency to split, there is no room for the seemingly negative to coexist with the seemingly positive, or for one person to exist alongside another: thus, she explains "they were my parents," not "they were *like* my parents." One eliminates the other.

At times, Yael's split causes her true feelings to be distorted or foreclosed:

> Y: ...He ate everything. My grandfather was also very anal about what he ate. Like, he had to have his toast black, and if it didn't come black, he'd send it back or would just get up and leave the restaurant. Like, I can't even tell you how many restaurants he's just gotten up and left and just like, "I'm not eating here." I thought it was endearing, like really endearing.
> N: He would get angry about little things like that?
> Y: Yeah, like he would... like he would be playing cards with his friends and one of his friends came over and got coy in Hebrew and he would be like, "Shalom." He would be like, "Oh, you think you know Hebrew, you big shot? How do you say 'give me an apple'?" He was that type of personality. Very rough and mean almost. He would yell

> a lot all the time… always screaming and yelling but in a funny way, not a really mean way…

Yael works hard to explain how it is possible that her grandfather was "mean" but at the same time not mean, screaming and yelling but in an "endearing" way. She gets stuck in her attempts to idealize *all* of him, working to present a man worthy of adoration, with no traceable flaw. Along the lines of this splitting, her grandfather's death represented the death of "everything": "I remember that for me, when my grandfather passed away, I lost everything… I lost my grandfather, I lost my father, I lost my best friend… like, I lost everything." Furthermore, because her grandfather and her grandfather's history are so much a part of her current existence, Yael struggles to inscribe the past as past.

> It wasn't just losing a grandfather; it was losing our rock and our stone and like kind of the person who would always tell us what to do. Does that make sense? He was just always the organizer of the family. At Passover Seders he would obviously be the leader… he wouldn't even know people's names and it wouldn't even matter. He would just be like, "You, read next." And then he would just like stop them, cut them off and be like, "You, next." That's how he would lead it—in a very rough way. And now, for my family ever since then, Seder is really, really hard because it's not as funny anymore.

Indeed, it's not "funny" how lost this family feels without its leader, its "rock," the man who told them "what to do." It is also not funny to be left behind with an array of unprocessed, unspoken feelings of rage, guilt, and shame that is often intertwined with family unity and pride. By no longer being told "what to do," this family has suddenly become vulnerable to thinking, feeling, and sprouting from a world of "stone."

Yael's family has spent three generations speaking about the Holocaust and attempting to create a meaningful life in the context of their collective trauma. The meaning they created was largely based on a continuance of Holocaust memory, whether through speeches, memorials, or recounting of stories. Unquestionably, their memories persevere. However, the work that remains for this family is the "feeling" work, the more difficult and threatening work that might cause one person to fall off a pedestal or another to individuate from the family. Yael arrives at the interview with a sense of hope, knowing her potential to honestly examine her role within the family, explore her "negative" feelings, and begin to live more fully as a separate individual within the present world. In verbalizing her own narrative, Yael impels herself to reflect on and blend the black and white extremes that can direct her life, and seek a more attainable shade of gray.

CHAPTER 6: REBECCA

Attempts at a "Rational" Life

> Well, (sigh) currently there's actually some significant issues going on because my grandfather is senile and has turned against my family. He's come to call my mother a Nazi. He refuses to talk to my mother or me because he sees me as the embodiment of her, talks only to my younger sisters and my father, and to them talks solely about how he hates my mother and how she wanted to lock him up in a nursing home. None of which is true—my mother only has his best interest at heart and if he allowed it she would go up and visit him whenever he wanted.

Davoine and Gaudillière (2004) address the above phenomenon by exploring "The revival of the catastrophes: the old people were sounding the alarm to us; we're in 1938: Munich; we're in 1939: the Blitzkrieg; we're in 1941: Pearl Harbor, and the United States is entering the war. Nothing will ever be the same anymore" (p. xviii). Instantaneously, one trauma embodies every trauma, one frightening situation transforms into every previous experience of fear. More comprehensively, Davoine and Gaudillière's psychological reactions to "traumatic breaks in the social link" include denial ("what happened didn't happen"), survival guilt ("Why them and not us?"), identification with the aggressor ("We had it coming"), perversion of judgment ("the victims were guilty and vice versa"), fascination with mass destruction, the aforementioned "revival of the catastrophes," and, lastly, "trivialization: the proliferation and sophistication of the commentaries going hand in hand with the anesthetizing of feelings" (2004, p. xvii-xviii).

For Rebecca, a 23-year-old, third generation descendant of two Holocaust survivors, some of the above reactions are apparent. While she indicates that her grandfather's stories have been obstructed from her knowledge, historically-relevant dynamics continue to be reenacted and transmitted along the generations of her family. Upon my asking about an event or an experience which may have triggered her grandfather's above accusations, Rebecca attempted to coherently organize the order of events:

> ...My mother made a comment. So he lives by himself in a community center. I don't know what it's like now; I haven't been there in two years. He was fully self-sufficient at the time. My mom said to him that for social reasons he might want to consider assisted living. My family probably knows more about this probably than the normal person because my dad is an elder care lawyer so we understand what these facilities are like; we're not trying to shove him away or anything like that. He took the suggestion in a completely different manner than what it was suggested and just started ranting about how we just wanted to lock him up and never see him again. And how we're not going to put him away, we're not going to lock him up like the Holocaust... and Hitler put him away and... afterwards he struck my mother. That's the story. We don't know where that came from and that was the point where he just started it.

"He just started it," Rebecca concludes, as though she is on trial for her grandfather's provocation. While she neutrally begins the story of that day with "my mother made a comment," this comment quickly evolves into a "suggestion" which he took "in a completely different manner than what it was suggested." Hesitantly, Rebecca reveals that assisted living was proposed, immediately following up this confession with a description of her family knowing "more about this probably than the normal person." She says, "my dad is an elder care lawyer so we understand what these facilities are like; we're not trying to shove him away or anything like that." On a surface level, Rebecca seems to be struggling with the notion that family members of an elder care lawyer know better about these "facilities" and would never "shove" anyone in. However, more deeply at play in this conflict is that Rebecca's family has assumed the role of aggressor in the face of a historically and personally pertinent, victim-perpetrator dynamic. She outwardly rejects, but simultaneously feels a part of, her grandfather's allegation. The discrepancy between conscious, rational logic and unconscious, irrational feelings quickly breaks down. Rebecca's total confusion, "We don't know where that came from," is thus understandable: how did she suddenly transform into a Nazi German? Is she deserving of this accusation? If not, what about this overwhelming sense of guilt that she has in some way brought about his past and present suffering?

Certainly, Rebecca does not need to prove that her mother is not a Nazi, not Hitler, and not in the habit of cruelly maltreating family members as was done to Jews in Nazi Germany. Her grandfather's past and present experiences are incomparable, and the context of person, place, and time has radically changed. Nevertheless, although rationally separate from Nazi imprisonment, Rebecca's grandfather suddenly finds himself in a conversation hinting at relocation, loss of independence, and an altered lifestyle. A world away from, yet at the same time never truly away from, Nazi Germany, Rebecca's grandfather suddenly finds his past and present collide. Instantaneously, he is back in a Holocaust world, and Rebecca's mother (and Rebecca, as her mother's "embodiment") are transformed into Nazis who "want to lock him up and never see him again." Rebecca herself speaks to the clash between the rational and the irrational:

> R: ...so it's actually a very difficult situation because my mother will say she's fine and we know she's not... and she spends a lot more time dwelling on it, much more than she should, because she doesn't work so we know she thinks about it a lot when she shouldn't. We've had a hard time trying to convince her that he is mentally not there. She doesn't seem to accept it.
> N: What does she think is going on?
> R: She tries to reason with him. Like, try to respond to his accusations with a rational answer, whereas he's not a rational person so it doesn't matter what you say back...

Similarly, Rebecca later recognizes that "being rational with someone who is mentally insane is just not going to get you anywhere." Yet what happens when an entire narrative, the overarching context for a person's past and present, is "mentally insane"? That is, in Rebecca's and her family's post-Holocaust life, nothing can ever again be simply sane. Therefore, by focusing on the fact that her senile grandfather cannot be reasoned with, Rebecca also stops short of exploring her own "insane" reactions to her grandfather and his story. As Danieli (1981, 1984) discusses in her work with Holocaust survivor patients, countertransferential issues with these individuals can take on terrifyingly powerful dimensions. Similarly, Rebecca's reactions to this cut-off, yet all-pervading moment in time with her grandfather are likely overwhelming: perhaps she feels immense guilt for his past experiences, for not having lived through the Holocaust herself, or for wanting to lock him up, like the Nazis did; she may be undergoing murderous rage at her grandfather for calling her a Nazi, for mobilizing her guilt, or for not rising above hostility and resentment himself; finally, Rebecca could be experiencing a combination of dread and horror, shame, grief and mourning—all countertransference themes described by clinicians working closely with descendants of Holocaust survivors (Danieli, 1981, 1984). Instead of exploring these possible feelings, however, Rebecca suggests that her family "shouldn't" dwell on the irrational but rather neglect or avoid them in what could become a "conspiracy of silence" (Danieli, 1984). She therefore forecloses an array of experiences, grasping at a more orderly sense of self. Ironically though not surprisingly, Rebecca's mother has a more difficult time chalking up the experience of being called a Nazi to her father's mental insanity; thus, Rebecca finds herself having "a hard time trying to convince her that he is mentally not there."

Feeling as though I was treading lightly so as not to overstep my boundaries and elicit anger or shame, I cautiously inquired about Rebecca's feelings surrounding her grandfather's attack:

> N: And has this been upsetting for you or have you been able to keep a distance from it and serve as a kind of rational voice for your mom?
> R: (Laughing) It's a weird question I guess because subconsciously... my sisters asked me a lot over the years. So, I completely understand that he's mentally insane and I understand that what's going on now is not normal, is not how a normal person would react because he's mentally not there. And my sister doesn't accept it;

> like, she'll talk to him and she'll just start hysterically crying and it will impact her whole day... happens like once a month when she talks to him, and my mother also will get incredibly upset about it. My father and I are fine. And I'm not sure if I'm just sub-consciously upset that I'm not consciously realizing it, or if I really am just really okay with the situation. Cause I feel fine with it. I'm not sure why. I'm just really fine with it. Like, I understand he's insane. It's a sad situation, but this is what happens. I'm not really sure. I think I'm okay with it ... I'm fine.

The "anesthetizing of feelings" referred to by Davoine and Gaudillière (2004) allows Rebecca to be "consciously" okay with the idea of her mother and her being called Nazis. The eldest daughter of three, and most apparently her mother's daughter, Rebecca wonders whether perhaps she is "sub-consciously upset," or if she is "just really okay with the situation." While she struggles out loud with the question of whether or not she is "fine," it becomes increasingly clear that she is, in fact, anything but fine: "My father and I are fine ... Cause I feel fine with it. I'm not sure why. I'm just really fine with it ... I'm not really sure. I think I'm okay with it ... I'm fine." This repetitive assertion that she is "fine," one that encouraged the interviewer not to question the declaration, established a barrier, tenuous but respected, between narrator and listener. Throughout this discussion, Rebecca's eloquence and refined mannerisms further enhanced her sane self-presentation. Nevertheless, Rebecca's previous declaration "my mother will say she's fine and we know she's not" reverberated throughout the interview, suggesting that Rebecca's externalized "we know she's not fine" may be a reflection of her own internal reality.

Day-to-Day Amidst the Irrational

In attempting to share his traumatic Holocaust experiences with his family, Rebecca's grandfather encountered an audience unable to serve as an audience. Rebecca reveals:

> Growing up, my mother said my grandparents... es-

> pecially my grandfather… wanted to talk a lot about his stories, which she didn't listen to, and her brother, Thomas, really refused to listen to. Her brother, Thomas, had an extremely bad relationship with his parents to the extent that he left home. They've had absolutely no contact with him over the years; he really cut them off when he was 18, and that was because my grandparents are very difficult to deal with, particularly my grandmother. But part of that was he just didn't want to deal with the stories and my grandparents always tried to press it on him.

The struggle of survivors attempting but failing to communicate their anguish has been commonly discussed in the Shoah literature, as have the various responses to such attempts. Danieli (1984) writes, "This conspiracy of silence is not confined to psychotherapists but is part of the conspiracy of silence that has characterized the interaction between survivors and society at large since the end of World War II" (p. 24). Interestingly, Rebecca's depiction of her family's unwillingness or inability to listen sheds light on her grandfather's "insane" explosion later in life, as the shut-out and buried experiences ultimately press for ex-press-ion. At the same time, it is likely that Rebecca's mother and uncle did a great deal of listening and containing growing up, engaging with the traumatic and traumatizing topic to such an extent that Holocaust history overwhelmed and overshadowed their present lives. Perhaps boundaries and separation were implemented as a final, concrete attempt at an existence somewhat liberated from the Holocaust. Maybe physical separation from their survivor parents served as their only hope for a life increasingly removed from the trauma.

The inability to communicate reappears throughout Rebecca's interview:

> Yeah, so my grandmother, she was really hard to communicate with… you couldn't have a conversation with her… I don't think she knew anything about me at all actually, you know in terms of what I was doing in school, who my friends were, what I liked doing… they would just sit and talk about like general stuff… they would

talk a lot about the weather, stuff like that, and we would play games with them but it was all very forced.

Rebecca expresses frustration regarding her inability to communicate with her grandmother and grandfather, whom she feels were generally limited to superficial topics, like the weather. Nevertheless, she wishes to be known by them, as an individual with friends, likes and dislikes, etc. The resulting communal experience in this family is therefore a sense of not being asked, not being heard, and ultimately, not being known; while her grandfather cannot impart his life story, Rebecca likewise encounters restrictions on what she can convey. Thus, although these family members share similar hopes and desires, they seem to exist within two separate worlds. Rebecca accounts for some of this disconnect by describing her grandparents' Holocaust community:

> R: There were a lot of Holocaust survivors in their community, so socially it became relatively isolated. Like, my grandfather worked; my grandmother was a fantastic real estate broker mainly because she was the pushiest thing you've ever met. She did pretty well there because of that. Socially, they just hung out with other Holocaust survivors who I think had similar mentalities. So, I think it was a reflection of adjusting and there just wasn't a big need to adjust.
> N: But they were trusting enough to maintain those relationships?
> R: Yes, within the Holocaust community. There's a very big difference between survivors and non-survivors there. Very big. All their friends were. All their friends were.

Rebecca emphasizes, "There's a very big difference between survivors and non-survivors." Indeed, the differences transcend age, language, and life experiences. Rebecca's grandparents cannot talk about their grandchild's friends, likes and dislikes, because they themselves were stripped of these benign childhood experiences. In her work, "I Was a Shoah Child," Yolanda Gampel writes of children in the Holocaust, "Through the creation of a 'false self' these children were able to function as adults, in the bodies of children, thereby enabling their survival. Inordinate capacities to struggle and to manage without the comfort of tears and teddy bears were evidenced by these child-adults" (1992, p. 391). While her "child-adult" grandparents attempt to cling to their superficial knowledge of a benevolent worldview, their treatment of every human encounter, every morsel of food, and every hug reflects an unadjusted mentality unfitting for the present time. Indeed, Rebecca's grandparents are in need of assistance in living in a post-Holocaust world. The "suggestion" made by Rebecca's mother was likely one of many attempts at reconnecting her disconnected father to humankind.

The void and hollow existence of a Holocaust survivor following this massive trauma could not be transmitted to Rebecca's mother or to Rebecca in a verbal capacity. While this is generally the case given that language is a superimposed phenomenon that serves as a distant substitute for the actual experience, the rejection of language was maximized in this family. Therefore, the dynamics of her grandparents' past experiences were acted out with family members instead, revealing themselves through familial interactions and relationships. For example, Rebecca's mother, who did not herself live as a Jew during Nazi Germany, nevertheless understands what it means to be assaulted and charged with an ambiguous crime; Rebecca's uncle, regardless of attempts to flee his history, knows first-hand what it means to be disjointed and isolated, somewhat like an orphan; finally, Rebecca can easily identify the experience of not being treated like a human. She recalls this type of environment:

> So, growing up, going there was just like... we hated it. We would go once every two or three months, and they live like two hours away from us in Maine and they always treated us like dolls; you know, they would just hug you and kiss you regardless of what you said or wanted, you had no actual opinion or no actual being, you were just a cute grandkid...

"You had no actual opinion or no actual being," Rebecca explains, an insignificant, lifeless "doll," outwardly appearing like a human but inwardly not alive. As Gampel (1992) writes, "In the face of the terrifying and traumatic reality of the Shoah, the ego of the Shoah child was

CHAPTER SIX

forced to function automatically and without expression of feeling" (p. 391). Indeed, a "doll" appears and performs in whatever manner desired by the holder of the doll, moving mechanically and without emotional expression. Similarly, Rebecca describes her grandmother's treatment of her mother by stating, "She always dressed my mother in skirts. My mother came home from college one day with a pair of jeans and my grandmother tore them up and threw them away." Again, we have a glimpse into the life of Rebecca's mother as a doll, dressed by her mother in skirts and unacknowledged as an individual with desires, feelings, and abilities. The boundary-less, intrusive treatment of people in this manner arose again in the context of food:

> We always went there and we always had a huge feast in front of us regardless of what time it was of the day and we were required to eat another huge feast like four hours later. There was a ridiculous amount of food around all the time and if we didn't absolutely stuff ourselves and then eat again four hours later and do the same thing we were just ridiculed. When I was younger, in elementary school, I was a small kid and my grandmother was worried to the extent that she called the nurse at my elementary school, pretended to be a social worker, and said to the nurse, "I'm calling as a social worker of the state. There's a student there, Rebecca. She is being abused— she's not being fed." And the nurse was a friend of my mother's and she understood that it was my mother's mom. So right away she called my mom and said, "I think your mother just called." So my mother was pretty upset about that, because she did some stuff like that.

Rebecca was "required to eat" whenever her grandparents played mealtime; however, the experience was anything but a game. She found herself forced to "absolutely stuff" herself, creating a physically visceral image of the human body as a plastic, manufactured entity. The connections to Rebecca's previous depiction of her grandmother as "the pushiest thing you've ever met" comes to mind, both because of the word "pushiest" and because of the description of a person as a "thing." Along these lines, in response to my question about her mother's ability to protect her in these situations, Rebecca replied:

> My mother would, but… I guess there wasn't a need for a barrier because all that really happened was we would go there and they would tell us how cute we were for a few hours. And then there'd be the whole food issue if we didn't eat like five helpings or fill our seven-year-old bodies.

Rebecca's grandmother, having survived Bergen-Belsen, is convinced that her granddaughter's thinness relates to "being abused" and "not being fed." She intervenes on her granddaughter's behalf, as if traveling back in time and saving herself from the starvation of the death camp. Through this muddled repetition and concretization of history, her grandmother acts out a chaotic attempt to undo her own past suffering. Yet in re-writing history such that someone could save her, her grandmother simultaneously winds up exploiting Rebecca and her mother. Understandably, as Rebecca says, her mother was "pretty upset about that."

The reserved, nonchalant description of anger as "pretty upset" is congruent with Rebecca's later ambivalent depiction of her mother's "harshness":

> R: I know she was brought up kind of under the stick more than the carrot strategy. I know she got into a lot of fights with her parents… she never specifically talked about their outbursts… she also only talks about what she wants to, which is just an issue with her in general, so there's a very big possibility that she decided that that's just something she's not going to talk about again, which I wouldn't be surprised about. She is definitely more strict with us than she's needed to be over the years, which has been tempered by my father because they balance each other out very well in that regard. And that's something that's been talked about between my father and myself and my sisters. My mother has a certain way of doing and if things aren't done that way she

CHAPTER SIX

> gets very annoyed.
> N: Like what?
> R: Nothing serious, she just has a much harsher tone of voice, and much more condescending than she needs to be... both to my sisters, myself, and my father. Generally given the circumstances surrounding whatever vent there is, there's absolutely no reason for it. I think that it is significantly less than what she faced growing up...

In Rebecca's use of the phrase "the stick more than the carrot strategy," she refers to her grandparents' utilization of punishment rather than reward. A number of interesting topics arise in this narrative, including a return to food; a tendency for her mother to "decide" what she wants to talk about and refrain from discussing other topics; and finally, her mother's "unnecessary" harsh and condescending tone with her immediate family. While Rebecca protectively suggests that this pattern is "nothing serious," she also reveals that it is serious enough to have been discussed by her father, her sisters, and herself. Furthermore, while she reminds herself that her mother's harshness is "significantly less than what she faced growing up," she nevertheless seems to be grappling with the fact that her mother has upsetting outbursts of anger that should be taken "serious." Rebecca continues to struggle with whether or not her mother's anger is a "big deal" in the subsequent exchange:

> R: A lot of my tendencies which I find naturally coming out are more towards my mother... my mother got annoyed when it wasn't a big deal and she got annoyed a lot...
> N: Little things?
> R: Not little things but... yeah, I guess. Things that she shouldn't have gotten annoyed about she would, and she would be much harsher in certain respects than she should have.
> N: Would she get angry?
> R: Not angry but basically like one harsh sentence and that would be it. It wasn't like a continual thing at all. She wouldn't yell or scream; it would just be like a much harsher tone of voice than was needed. Growing up, it

was something I got used to. My youngest sister is significantly younger than me, she's 14, so when I go home and see that every time it happens, I'm just shocked to realize that's how things are done... which we're trying to work on as well with her.
N: So it's out in the open?
R: We're trying to make it that way. Yeah, she's definitely harsher than she should be.

Rebecca states "it wasn't a big deal," but understandably feels uncomfortable with my labeling the triggers for her mother's anger as "little things." By explaining that her mother "shouldn't" have been annoyed or was harsher than she "should" have been, there is a sense that Rebecca maintains a certain impression of how a mother "should" or "should not" behave. That is, she *should* not be "angry," she *should* not "yell or scream," and in the case that she does, it *shouldn't* be a "continual thing." It seems that Rebecca's primary struggle surrounds her own feelings of anger and aggression, further shedding light on her discomfort in the role of the Nazi aggressor with her grandfather. She concludes, "we're trying to work on that as well with her" and "we're trying to make it that way," clearly indicating her recognition that something has to change. This attempt to open up a dialogue about her mother's impact on the family may ultimately be personally constructive for Rebecca as well; after all, she notices that many of her tendencies "naturally coming out" are similar to her mother's. It seems that Rebecca has been able to broach the long-avoided, frightening conversation of family dynamics, acknowledge the sometimes uncomfortable patterns, and initiate a potential for change.

CHAPTER 7: SAMANTHA

Holocaust Trauma: One, Two, Three Generations

S: So he, um, was born in Poland in Bialystok and he had a mom and a dad and I believe two sisters, and all of them were killed in the war. And my grandfather himself was in the concentration camp; he was in Auschwitz. He might have also been in other ones but I'm not sure. And he... when America liberated the concentration camps, he came to America. Anyway, they ended up in New York, and he met my grandmother and... um... let's see... actually, that's like a whole other story because my grandmother was never diagnosed but I think she was Bipolar amongst God knows what other mental illnesses she had. So, my grandfather himself was obviously very affected by the war and the combination of the two of them was not good and they just made each other sicker and my mom's childhood was really difficult and I think that the war had a huge impact on my mom and on me...
N: In what way?
S: In her house, it was.... (long silence). I guess I've just been told bits and pieces but I know something that could have come from the war or that I could relate to it in my head is that they used to make my mom eat and drink milk when she was full and she didn't want anymore. And they like forced her... so she would hide food that she didn't want to eat in her closet. Now that I'm even talking about it, not only is it probably relevant but it's like the opposite of that happened for my grandfather because you know, they didn't have food.
N: You say now that you talk about it, have you thought about it before, for example, the food?
S: I've thought about the food and the fact that because my grandfather probably was starving... and the com-

bination of that with my grandmother's weird issues with food… and then they were weird with food with my mom. But I never thought about the fact that it was so like, the fact that she was hiding food in her closet when she was a little girl was literally like the opposite of my grandfather probably like starving.

Samantha, the 31-year-old granddaughter of a Holocaust survivor, delves into a number of issues often tentatively mentioned by Holocaust descendants only moments into her interview. She touches on mental illnesses, the emergence of patterns through the generations, the "huge" impact of the war on all three generations, and the ongoing struggle surrounding food. "…he had a mom and a dad and I believe two sisters," she says, individually listing each murdered family member rather than clumping them into the category "family," or more specifically, "parents and siblings." In this way, each family member is separately acknowledged. She goes on to relate her mother's relationship with food to that of her grandfather, stating, "…the fact that she was hiding food in her closet when she was a little girl was literally like the opposite of my grandfather probably like starving." Samantha elucidates the link between starvation and not having food on the one hand, with hoarding and ensuring an ongoing supply of food on the other. Indeed, having versus not having to some extent represent opposites: opposites so intimately connected through this family's past experiences that they begin to coalesce into one mutually-defining entity. After all, hunger alone delineates the experience of being full, and hoarding implies a fear of not having in the future. As her mother hid the food that she did not want to eat in the closet—instead of throwing it out or giving it away—she behaved the way her father might have behaved in Auschwitz had he stumbled upon a supply food: eat some now and save the rest for later.

Annie Rogers writes in the opening personal anecdote of her novel, *The Unsayable: The Hidden Language of Trauma*:

> I had always been attracted to heights—tall rocks, fire escapes, trees, and precipices. As I teetered at the edge of the school roof, I did not know that my father had actually committed suicide. He'd jumped and fallen five stories to his death … My mother finally told me this af-

ter the art teacher called and informed her of my sojourn on the school roof (2007, p. 14).

Similarly, Samantha's mother likely understood her hiding of food as an attempt to avoid excessive, forced eating; in Samantha's words, "And they like forced her... so she would hide food that she didn't want to eat in her closet." However, in the midst of discussing this behavior, Samantha is able to arrive at an intergenerational viewpoint, an outlook which gives further meaning to her mother's tendencies and anchors it in history. The mutually defining "opposites" are thereby linked as counterparts, exposed over two generations, in two different worlds, offering a here and now observation of what happened *there*. That is, Samantha's openness and insight allow her to recognize her mother's reenactment of her grandfather's concentration camp experiences. Samantha continues:

> Um, my grandparents, both of them had multiple suicide attempts. They were always taking pills and going into hospitals. My grandfather I think somatized a lot of his mental anguish and um... he was physically sick but I think a good percentage of his physical illness was really mental because he would go to the hospital and they would say there was nothing wrong. But he was sick and when I really think about it... he had this thing called scleroderma, and I'm not sure exactly what that is but I know he had it his whole life. And as he got older, he kind of looked like 20 years older than he was, and towards the end of his life he looked like he was 90 but I think he was 70. And there were a few years where he could only whisper. I don't know if that was like... now that I think about it now, it probably was mental. But at the time it seemed like some sort of a physical thing. For years he only whispered when he spoke. And what else did he do... he could only eat mushy food... he had a lot of digestive, a lot of digestive issues. Um... and he... when I got a little bit older he would try to talk to me about the war but he would always end up crying. And I think I was too young to understand so I didn't really appreciate what he was telling me, and also it would bother

me. I would be like, "I don't want to go visit him, he's just gonna cry and then I'm gonna cry and I don't wanna do that." But now that I'm older, I understand what he was trying to talk to me about.

As the descriptions of her grandfather's life pour out of Samantha, overwhelming us with stories of suicide attempts, hospitals, and illnesses, we begin to have a sense of the engulfing and overpowering nature of these experiences on her upbringing. Nevertheless, she speaks honestly about these incidents, exploring her grandfather's limitations as well as her own inability to bear witness to his past trauma. "My grandfather I think somatized a lot of his mental anguish ... I think a good percentage of his physical illness was really mental because he would go to the hospital and they would say there was nothing wrong." The need to somatize his mental anguish expresses her grandfather's inability to *do* something with his grief; to verbalize it or sublimate it or work through it in some way. As Cyrulnik (2005) writes,

> The most common emergency defense mechanism is the symptom, an observable phenomenon expressing a part of the invisible inner world. As soon as the symptom illustrates the pulverization of the internal world, the person can pinpoint an image for his own unhappiness and hence feels better. He knows where the pain comes from and can finally give a name to it (p. 101).

It seems Samantha's grandfather's pain took the form of many names—whether scleroderma, digestive issues, or literally an inability to speak—all elements of something terrible and inarticulate.

Faced with the medical opinion that "there was nothing wrong" with him, Samantha's grandfather descended deeper and deeper into his tortured internal world. Samantha's recollection that "For years he only whispered when he spoke" provides a concretized example of an existence hanging somewhere in-between attempts at language and the inevitable, "unsayable" nature of his experiences. Unfortunately, though understandably, the murmurs of memory are often met with a refusal to take in—a reluctance to join in the suffering: "...I didn't really appreciate what he was telling me, and also it would bother me. I would be like, 'I don't want to go visit him, he's just gonna cry and then I'm gonna cry and I don't wanna do that.'" Unable to verbally share his war experiences with his family, her grandfather's tears poured out of him, flailing for release. Ultimately, barely comprehensible through whispers and tears, his memories were forced underground and registered physically instead.

The physicality of her grandfather's suffering reappears in Samantha's later discussion of her grandmother's physical abuse of him:

> N: So was he ever diagnosed? Was he hospitalized psychiatrically?
> S: I don't really know, in my family a lot of things were hidden, especially when we were younger. So I know he was in the hospital a lot of times and I'm assuming some of it was psychiatric. There was abuse between my grandmother... my grandmother I think used to physically abuse him.
> N: Oh, wow.
> S: So, I don't know really the extent of that, but I was told at one point that towards the end of their life... my mom said something like that she hit—my grandmother hit him with a menorah, and um, something about him falling out of bed or she pushed him out of bed or something. And he was so sick at the end, he had cancer, he had bone cancer in his stomach and bones, and then um... I was gonna say something else about the abuse but I forget what it was.
> N: Did your mom ever get abused?
> S: I don't know. She always says there were always things flying in the house. So I think things that my grandmother was probably throwing. She might have been hit, I don't know. Um, I was gonna say something else about... *oh*, what I was gonna say was that my mother told me when I was older after my grandfather had died that he, that my grandmother had abused him for years but that he never told anyone and never told my mother because he was so ashamed. Um (silence)... this is really depressing.

In contemplating and organizing facts that she "knows" from those she "assumes," we get a sense that Samantha is constructing a narrative for herself for the first time. While she first suggests she does not "know really the extent of that," she later recalls, "*oh*, what I was gonna say was that my mother told me... that he, that my grandmother had abused him for years but that he never told anyone and never told my mother because he was so ashamed." As soon as she "remembers" having been told this information by her mother, Samantha falls silent, then truthfully discloses, "this is really depressing." It is no wonder that knowledge of her grandfather's abuse and silent shame are momentarily "forgotten," as blocking them out serves to protect Samantha, and the remainder of the family, from experiencing the ensuing "depressing" feelings. Thus, for a moment, she chooses not to "know really" and reaches for a concealing safety net with the statement "in my family a lot of things were hidden." Moments later, Samantha discloses much more than expected: she reflects on her experience in the moment, sits with the weight of the pain, and then reassures the interviewer, "I think it's good to talk about it, but it's just like *ugh*..." In a sense, Samantha communicates, "This is hard work, but I am able and willing to do it."

Interestingly, Samantha's mother began to divulge information about her own father only after his passing. Perhaps with his death, the search for truth was ignited. More likely, however, Samantha's mother could no longer contain the family secrets on her own, and spilled onto her daughter to help carry the load. That is, while family dynamics and historical memory had been transmitted nonverbally to Samantha throughout her life, she was additionally elected as the conscious, verbal beneficiary of family narrative. It is unsurprising that Samantha struggles to organize the lines between fantasy and reality, certainty and uncertainty; after all, her mother's attempts to reveal and conceal information overlapped throughout her childhood, creating a hazy, muddled grasp on what could be counted as true. Samantha goes on to describe seemingly contradictory but nevertheless coexisting experiences of withholding secrecy and a violation of boundaries that characterized the chaotic atmosphere of her childhood home:

> S: ...I think "oh, it's just because I was a child," or "you don't tell your children that," or "we had things when we were children..." But I definitely think that in my family,

> with my parents, we were never told when the grandparents were sick or when something bad happened, or we were told a few weeks later. I even remember that once my dad passed out and he went to the hospital and my parents didn't tell me until the next day. And I was so mad, like I just feel like that's not fair. And at that point I was an adult.
> N: So they thought you couldn't handle hearing it?
> S: Yeah, they didn't want to burden me with it... which I guess I do understand if you're a child. So I feel like I was never told all these things and then when I became older it started. My mom started to tell me all these crazy things about her family...

"...and then when I became older it started," says Samantha, recalling a turning point in her life in which silence and secrecy were replaced by boundary-less spilling of personal anecdotes and feelings. It is unclear when and why the transition occurred. However, it seems that Samantha was confronted with both excessive secrecy and excessive disclosure in adulthood, creating an erratic and unpredictable environment for her. In either scenario, Samantha's lack of control and stability is palpable: she remains blindly uninformed when her father spends a night in the hospital, yet is asked to contain all the "crazy" details about her extended family. She is left bewildered, feeling she never "had things" when she was a child; after all, "having" implies retaining something at least relatively consistent. The chaotic atmosphere of her childhood is further revealed through Samantha's discussion of the intergenerational transmission of trauma through three generations of her family:

> N: So how do you think the way your mother was raised impacted her as a mother? Do you see that in her?
> S: Yeah. She could have used like 20 years of therapy. But I think she's afraid to really touch on anything. So she never, she always was afraid. She didn't tell me she was afraid, but I think she was afraid. I think it impacted us a lot—we used to fight a lot. Also, it really affected me when I was a child because... my mom

was a young mother; she was 24 when she had me. And she was taking care of her parents because they always depended on her. So she was always getting calls about what's wrong, just complaining about all these different health issues, and um… I think it was more than I was saying. I think they would call her and say things about their bowel movements and there were enemas… just like, weird, weird things going on. And they would always get sick and have to go to the hospital or they were swallowing pills, so she was kind of raising me and my sister but she was also running around taking care of them. And I don't think that she… I think there was a way that she could have addressed that and lived with that if she could have gotten help that would have prevented it from taking over her life. But instead, she totally allowed it to take over. Plus, whatever issues she and my dad were having… obviously, her upbringing affected her choice in relationship with my dad and my dad wasn't always the most supportive husband, or I should say the most active husband. Like, he went to work and that was his job. According to what my mom says he was never very active in child rearing and household things and other things like that. So I think in a lot of ways he was missing emotionally and physically. So she was taking care of us and she was taking care of her parents, and I think she was pissed, and I think she took a lot of it out on me.
N: So you had to deal with her anger a lot.
S: Yeah.
N: And did she hit you? Was there abuse in your house?
S: Not chronically, but there were a few instances that I do recall with her hitting me. She definitely didn't hit me all the time, but she did scream at me all the time. And I definitely think there was some form of emotional… like, I definitely feel that I did not look to her as a support, I was more fearful of her when I was growing up. I think a lot has changed since then, but still, you carry that with you forever…

> N: Is your grandmother still alive?
> S: No, she committed suicide closely after my grandfather died. She went bonkers and took a bunch of pills.

Samantha's ability to reflect on her chaotic childhood experiences and early relationships is remarkable. She suggests, "I think there was a way that she could have addressed that and lived with that if she could have gotten help that would have prevented it from taking over her life. But instead, she totally allowed it to take over." Indeed, Samantha is simultaneously acknowledging her own journey to "address" it and prevent it from "taking over" her life. In what might have been an overwhelming presentation of a family narrative for a one-hour interview, Samantha's insight and awareness instead provided a certain sense of hope and growth during and following the hour. While her mother's raw, unprocessed, and consuming emotions encouraged her not to "really touch on anything" throughout her life, Samantha sought to achieve the opposite. She begins by emphasizing her mother's debilitating fear: "She didn't tell me she was afraid but I think she was afraid"; as well as her mother's escalating anger that mounted into explosive rage: "So she was taking care of us and she was taking care of her parents, and I think she was pissed, and I think she took a lot of it out on me." Furthermore, Samantha is not limited by shame or humiliation when discussing boundary-less revelations in her family: "I think it was more than I was saying. I think they would call her and say things about their bowel movements and there were enemas… just like, weird, weird things going on." That is, she is able to recognize and discuss the most difficult and the most "weird, weird things," thereby eliminating the power of silence and creating space for introspection.

Perhaps it is no coincidence that Samantha's grandfather married a woman who abused him, or that her mother chose a non-supportive, passive husband. Given their traumatic histories and the workings of family dynamics, aspects related to partner choice, food-related issues, and the foreclosure of feelings trickled down through the generations. Furthermore, silence surrounding their histories debilitated their chance of working through the past and establishing a place within the present. Thus, the first and second generations of Holocaust survivors found themselves enacting past traumas, adopting roles previously despised, and finding release around aggression but never understanding why. In discussing her own physical and emotional abuse by her mother, Samantha acknowledges the incessant power of early experiences, stating, "I was more fearful of her when I was growing up. I think a lot has changed since then, but still, you carry that with you forever…" We are therefore left with a number of questions: How many generations will receive this traumatic history? Does examining her history, her early relationships, and her inherent predispositions alter Samantha's course, splitting her path from that of her ancestors? Or will Samantha forever remain on the same course, working instead to recognize where she came from, where she is going, and how to more fully live her life along the way?

First Glimpses into Generation Number Four

> N: Going back a little, you mentioned your mom being really angry as a result of how she grew up. I'm wondering how that plays out for you in terms of anger.
> S: Yeah, well her anger was never really expressed in a modulated form. It was either explosive or covered over by anxiety, and God knows what else it's covered over by. And one of my issues in my therapy was working on expressing my anger, because before I was in therapy I did not allow myself to get angry because when I did it felt like… deadly or something. Because of the way I experienced it when I was younger. So I had to learn that anger is okay. You can be angry without killing someone (laughing).

While she laughs at the seemingly obvious statement that a person can be angry without killing someone, this realization has clearly been a major accomplishment for Samantha. Having experienced anger and aggression that was never "modulated" throughout her childhood, anger that was either "explosive or covered over by anxiety," Samantha's own expression of anger felt loaded and "deadly" for a long time. Through what she calls "life changing" therapy, she discovered that "anger is okay," clearly opening up her world to the possibility of tolerating this emotion and surviving its intensity. Learning to deal with anger,

CHAPTER SEVEN

however, was only one of many battles for Samantha, who regularly fears engaging in some of her predecessors' family patterns. For example, she recalls the onset of panic attacks surrounding major events in her life, such as the engagement to her husband and the birth of her baby boy:

> And then... we were engaged and we were gonna get married and I was having a lot of anxiety, like trouble breathing. And I think it had a lot to do with getting married and not re-doing my parents' relationship... I was like, okay, I have to go to therapy. And I stayed in that therapy for two and a half years and that was I think the most impactful therapy. And then, when I had Taylor and I was having panic attacks, I went back for a brief time. That was pretty brief. I think I was more sleep deprived than anything.

The fear of "re-doing" her parents' relationship, of becoming a wife or a mother like her mother, is consistently on her mind. Samantha later describes her panic attacks as, "It would feel like I couldn't get a full breath. It wasn't a full-fledged panic attack. I was breathing but it felt like the air wasn't satisfying me." Understandably, her unremitting attempts to not recreate the past, and the ongoing awareness and determination to do things differently in the present, can be altogether exhausting. As Samantha begins to describe never getting "a full breath," feeling that the "air wasn't satisfying" her, it seems that the struggle to break away from historically entrenched family patterns requires a "full-fledged" attempt: every last breath is devoted to this cause, and every new breath is assessed for intergenerational meaning. As I asked Samantha about whether or not she reflects on herself as a mother, she responded emphatically, "Every... day":

> N: So do you think sometimes about yourself as a mother and how you want to be with your children and what you would want to differently?
> S: Every... day I think about that. I mean, I definitely try to take the good stuff that my parents gave me and do the bad stuff differently. I'm very conscious of not

losing my cool, not yelling, not taking out my anger on him. If I'm angry at something, at Jacob my husband, or whatever, just putting it off till later. Not being so impulsive and just really recognizing the importance… recognizing the importance of being a full support for him and taking care of him and not ever being a scary… I used to be scared when I would hear my mom's footsteps down the hall and I don't ever want him to feel like that. I want him to come snuggle with me and to know that I love him unconditionally. I know logically that my mom loves me unconditionally and has, but the way that I was growing up it felt like her love was not unconditional. When she got angry, it felt like I was totally abandoned.
N: How was it giving birth to your son and becoming a mother and that whole transition?
S: That was probably the hardest thing that I have ever done. I mean, after I had him, I had panic attacks. I don't know how much of it was hormones and how much of it was mental, probably some combination of both. But I was so scared. I did not know what to do with him. I mean, I've never been like a baby person. And then on top of everything, I think I was just so scared of re-doing everything… But I think I was so aware of it that I'm fine. And it's gotten so much better, like I'm fine now. But I think the beginning of being a mom was super, super hard. And I think probably has a lot to do with my own growing up.
N: Was there anything specific that was hard?
S: Feeding was hard because he was kind of colic-y and I think he had acid reflux and I had to switch his formula like five times and he was constipated so we had to have prune juice and he was spitting up a lot. But he always ate, so that was okay. (Silence.) It is just interesting thinking about when you're feeding your newborn baby, you want them to eat. But I think I am very aware of… because of everything that happened with my mom and forcing, he eats what he wants to eat and if he stops eating I just assume that he's not hungry…

CHAPTER SEVEN

In her attempts to do things differently from her parents and grandparents, Samantha to a large extent succeeds. She works hard not to become a "scary" figure to her husband and child, and to provide them with the unconditional love she felt she lacked growing up. She suggests that recognizing her fears, hopes, and desires has been the key: "But I was so scared. I did not know what to do with him... And then on top of everything I think I was just so scared of re-doing everything... But I think I was so aware of it that I'm fine," she says, and indeed there is a sense that her self-reflection allows her to pinpoint her weaknesses and reach out for help when necessary. Of course, each decision she makes, whether in parenting or in her marriage, is linked to an entire history of decisions—ones she might circumvent, and ones she might not. For example, Samantha describes consciously struggling with her baby's eating habits: on the one hand, she says, "you want them to eat," but on the other, "because of everything that happened with my mom and forcing, he eats what he wants to eat and if he stops eating I just assume that he's not hungry..." Each decision and behavior is consciously (and unconsciously) linked to her history, thereby allowing her to feel she "addressed that and lived with that." Similarly, in describing her choice in partner, Samantha reveals the changes through the generations:

> He's like a super-involved husband and father. And it's very equal in our relationship, like we both do everything. Like, he cooks, and he totally spends so much time with Taylor and takes care of him. On the weekends, I have to do homework pretty much all day and it's just like him and Taylor.

Despite, or perhaps because of, the numerous transformations she has willfully sought and achieved in her life, Samantha's day-to-day existence and moment-to-moment decisions inevitably summon her history. Whether she is feeding the baby, driving her car, or crossing the street, she experiences a combination of fear and gratitude:

> S: I definitely have had thoughts... I was thinking about it this morning as I was getting ready... it has to do with

everything that's going on in the world today, but it probably also has to do with the Holocaust… just like the fear. I would have these fears after I had the baby… well, I think about how lucky I am a lot. How lucky I am to live in America and how lucky I am that I have food and a house and a car and I go to school. And yet I just feel like I couldn't really be any luckier in terms of those things. And then I just think, like I've had a couple of thoughts, like fears… oh, maybe it was the World Trade Center that made me think about it. But just like, at any moment, what if somebody came and took away Taylor? And, again, I think I had these thoughts when he was a baby and I was feeding him his bottles… and what if something ever happened where there was some kind of thing that happened like a war or some kind of attack, and I couldn't get out of the house and get food for him? Like he would be starving. Or something about having my freedom and my power taken away, or having him taken away from me or something happening to him, or him being hungry or just how horrible that would be. That would be like the worst thing.

N: A lot of third generations talk about fear of death and loss.

S: Yeah, I think a lot of moments sometimes during the day I just think about that everything could really just end. A bus could hit me, lightning could strike me, war could break out—anything could happen. Usually, like 99% of the time, that gives me a good feeling… a feeling like I have to appreciate this moment, and I have to appreciate all the moments I've had up until now. You just never know. And we're all gonna die someday anyway, so just appreciating my freedom and everything I have. Kind of like an every day gift.

Alongside a historically-pertinent recognition that life cannot be taken for granted, Samantha describes the fears that accompany each day, causing her to "appreciate this moment" and "appreciate all the moments I've had up until now." She engages with some the most frightening questions and scenarios: "something about having my freedom and my power taken away, or having him taken away from me or something happening to him, or him being hungry or just how horrible that would be." In facing these fears rather then leaving them untouched and unexamined, Samantha also attains gratitude and the sense of "an every day gift." It is *through* her link with history that she more fully lives in the present.

CHAPTER 8: RUTH

Shame… or Pride

R: When I was in Madrid… I spent a semester in Madrid my junior year of college… I lived with this very, very old woman for like two days. She was like 90. Then I moved in with another family… it was a young mother and two daughters. I was gonna move again, so whatever, it's fine. But I noticed on the table after being there for a few weeks… it had different tiles on it… and one of the tiles in the center was a swastika. I was 20 years old and in a foreign country and I basically… I don't want to say that I hid the fact that I was Jewish, but I really tried to avoid the conversation. To me even, and that's not, look… that's nine or eight years ago. *I can't believe that I did that.* It's embarrassing to me that I didn't say something to someone at the time. And I remember asking her about it much later, right before I was leaving to come back to D.C., because I felt like I didn't know what was going to happen to me. She told me it was some like witch symbol or something and it wasn't what I thought it was. I guess it doesn't really matter, but that, like, we're talking about 2000.
N: I guess she didn't want to talk about it.
R: I know, it's crazy.
N: So you lived there.
R: I lived there. I lived there for five months (laughing).
N: You ate on that table.
R: Yeah. (Silence.) If that was me today I can't imagine being there for more than five minutes without saying something or leaving or doing something else.
N: I think it speaks to how hard it is to approach that topic.
R: It's very hard. Look, there's certain times when you feel

it's easier to not say something than to say something, and the fact that that goes on only proves the point that there are people who are anti-Semitic and people don't feel like they're thought of equally. To be ashamed or to hide the fact that you're Jewish from someone, the fact that that goes on today, is terrifying to me.

The 28-year-old granddaughter of two Holocaust survivors, Ruth reveals feeling ashamed for having been silenced in the face of a swastika. "I can't believe that I did that," she emphasizes, "It's embarrassing to me that I didn't say something to someone at the time." What might Ruth have said or done to alter the event or subsequent feelings about the event? Should she have engaged in a dialogue about anti-Semitism, the meaning of the swastika, or the injustice of history? Could she have tackled the reality of racism in the modern world, demanding an explanation for this woman's anti-Semitic beliefs, or even more ambitious: attempted to change this woman's opinion? Had Ruth revealed the fact that she was Jewish, might she have served as an example of a "normal" Jew, merely a young woman like any other, not at all someone to be feared or hated? Or might she have felt some relief in revealing her Jewish identity, even if this meant she was not "thought of equally," because she served as a living, breathing memorial for her murdered ancestors? How much of history can one person take on?

If history cannot be undone and sometimes "it's easier to not say something than to say something," why not remain silent? What is the value of broaching "that topic"? In Ruth's case, her past silence continues to plague her: "If that was me today I can't imagine being there for more than five minutes without saying something or leaving or doing something else." In essence, she is saying, "If that was me today I would not have been silenced by shame." She struggles to rationalize her silence with the fact that she considered making a change: "I was gonna move again, so whatever, it's fine"; and attempts to expunge the intensity of the topic altogether: "I guess it doesn't really matter." However, she is horrified and embarrassed by her experience of shame, as the feeling implies the presence of something to be ashamed *of*. She concludes, "To be ashamed or to hide the fact that you're Jewish from someone, the fact that that goes on today, is terrifying to me." That is, silence and humiliation about her background are "terrifying," given that millions were tortured and murdered for what was considered a "shameful" identity, while others stood silently by.

Although she regrets it, keeping her background a secret seemed to protect Ruth from experiencing an extensive sense of loss and anguish in a setting that might have undermined her painful history. She says, "I remember asking her about it much later, right before I was leaving to come back to D.C., because I felt like I didn't know what was going to happen to me," implying a two-sided fear: of an internal breakdown in defenses and of an external attack. Indeed, there is always the question of choosing to speak versus remaining silent. At the same time, however, speech that is driven by the pressure to prove oneself and the need to represent an entire history of a people might similarly (though perhaps successfully) divert attention from a person's underlying shame. Thus, while silence may appear to be the weaker, dishonorable counterpart of language, shame can exist in both speech and silence.

How Ruth might react in a similar situation eight or nine years later we cannot know. However, reflections on her past silence have driven her adult identity. She has attempted to transform her shame into pride, standing tall and strong, becoming self-sufficient and accomplished, and proving to the world that there is nothing to hide:

> R: ...the strength of a person, you know... there's nothing that I would want anybody to do for me because I feel like I can do it for myself. The same way my grandmother is, the same way my mothers is, sort of taking ownership and...
> N: Do for you... what kinds of things?
> R: Anything at all. The idea that you have to be not just independent but able to really survive on your own from, you know, emotionally, physically, financially, and maybe especially as a female... that may be a little bit of a different mentality but it's not... I'm not sure how to even describe it... my grandmother is probably, I mean, she's stubborn to no end but one of the most strongest human being I've ever encountered, and my mom's the same way; I mean, almost difficult to a point, right? My dad's biggest challenge is trying to do anything for her because she does everything by herself. My mother had

> more of a sense of guilt that she always felt she always had to do for her mother because of what they went though. I don't think I have that at all. I feel more of a responsibility to carry on being... having a Jewish family than anything, which I feel like for my mother was just a given. You know, that generation, obviously they were gonna marry somebody Jewish. For us it's now kind of more in the air. So that's something that to me is very important.

"I feel more of a responsibility to carry on being..." she trails off, clearly referring to a responsibility to carry on being a Jew. Given the struggle between shame and pride, silence and language, perceived weakness and strength, carrying on her Jewish identity is understandably a complex and loaded responsibility. She depicts the "strength of a person ... the same way my grandmother is, the same way my mothers is, sort of taking ownership and..." "Ownership," she suggests, implying the act of possessing and acknowledging her characteristics. For example, in "taking ownership" of who she is, Ruth might say, "This is mine" or "This is me." Thus, her confident depiction involving the "strength of a person" stands in contrast to her previous remark, "I don't want to say that I hid the fact that I was Jewish, but I really tried to avoid the conversation." Has Ruth worked through her past shame—examining, questioning, and exploring it—such that she now carries a sense of pride and ownership in its place? Or has shame been camouflaged by pride, as the two coexist on a continuum that is influenced by person, time, and place? Having been shaken by the discovery of a debilitating sense of shame, it seems that Ruth acquired a determination to rework this emotion and modify its role in her present identity.

Ruth attempts to explain the meaning of the "strength of a person," stating, "there's nothing that I would want anybody to do for me because I feel like I can do it for myself." Interestingly, in later describing her grandmother's concentration camp survival, Ruth divulges having written a school paper about the notion of "camp sisters": "It was about how people survived through a safety of having a sister. It wasn't typically a sister—could've been the most random person. Just that yin-yang kind of balance of pulling each other through... creating that kind of family..." While Ruth recognizes her grandmother's need for the support of another person in order to survive the camps, Ruth herself has worked to consciously eliminate the need for support from anyone. It seems Ruth's "strength of a person" relates to her past shame; in not wanting anyone to do anything for her and feeling like she can do it herself, she hopes to prove that the frightened, humiliated girl of eight years ago is gone. Her internal sense of self, therefore, continues to be driven by her individual and collective history, by her naturally arising shame, and by her disapproval of this emotion. In response to shameful affects, and her ongoing embarrassment about previous inaction, Ruth demands of herself unwavering pride and "strength": never again will she be the silent, frightened, 20-year-old student in a foreign country; never again will she feel anything but proud of her Jewish heritage; never again will she be the timid granddaughter of Holocaust survivors who is understandably stifled by the horrific truths of history. Never again.

But Ever-Present... Fear

Towards the conclusion of the interview, Ruth reveals that she no longer tears up during interviews like this one, while in the past she likely would have cried. The following conversation arose from this recognition:

> N: So how is it to sit here and talk about it and notice that you're not crying?
> R: I don't know. Maybe in some ways after being... you know, you get yourself to a certain point and I've always been someone who can create distance. You know, you've sort of got that emotional guard, like, I keep this here and compartmentalize it a little bit. So, I'm sure there's some of that. And I was also just... I don't even want to call it an acceptance, but it's kind of like you see this reality of what it is and it's kind of like there's nothing you can do about it but to move forward with the knowledge and the strength of what has happened and make sure the people around me don't forget. And maybe the next generation everyone will see each other as equal, but I don't know.
> N: So have you always had the ability to compartmentalize, or has that developed more recently?

R: No, that's old news.
N: You just kind of realized you were able to put distance between things?
R: Daughter of a psychologist.
N: Were you in therapy?
R: 24 hours a day (laughing). No, never.

Establishing a distance and compartmentalizing various aspects of her life have allowed Ruth to maintain what she calls an "emotional guard." She says, "I don't even want to call it an acceptance, but it's kind of like you see this reality of what it is and it's kind of like there's nothing you can do about it but to move forward with the knowledge and the strength of what has happened and make sure the people around me don't forget." Ruth attains a sense of strength in her "acceptance" of the past, feeling there is nothing she can "do" about it except make a place for history and ensure that historical realities are transmitted to future generations. However, reaching a level of acceptance required developing an emotional guard and an ability to compartmentalize her feelings; again, a reference to Ruth limiting certain experiences in order to maintain "strength." Furthermore, her use of humor allows Ruth to find relief in the intensity of her experiences. Yet, her feelings of fear, shame, and pride become less compartmentalized and increasingly hazy in the face of a 13-year-old boy's questioning of historical facts:

> To me, at this point more than anything, I see it... because I see so many people, especially like dating/marrying people who are not Jewish... and to me, most importantly, I feel like that would be disrespectful and not continuing the importance and the strength of how I identify, and how much of my family was killed, and so many of those issues that to me create a really strong force and desire to have a Jewish family and Jewish children and to teach them. And it scares me because I think there is a lot of forgetting that is about to go on. I have a 13-year-old cousin in L.A., who I saw a couple weeks ago, and he told me a kid in his school got punched in the face because he said the Holocaust never happened. And my guess is that that is like the tip of the iceberg in that you

> know my children's generation, our children's generation, will have a real uphill battle in terms of identifying themselves as Jews in many ways. And I think that the way I see myself as the granddaughter of Holocaust survivors... I don't see if that... I don't know if my children will feel as I felt. I think a lot of that generation will never know or touch a survivor the way a lot of us have.

While she hesitantly suggests the possibility that in "the next generation, everyone will see each other as equal," Ruth's ongoing fear and vulnerability continue to influence her day-to-day life. She says, "I see so many people, especially like dating/marrying people who are not Jewish... and to me, most importantly, I feel like that would be disrespectful and not continuing the importance and the strength of how I identify..." Ruth speaks to the commonly-held view of intermarriage as the greatest threat to the survival of Judaism—a modern-day form of annihilation anxiety. Furthermore, she struggles to depict "the importance and the strength" of her identity in contrast to her brothers, who "live under a different set of rules: one of them is married to someone who isn't Jewish, one of them probably will marry someone who's not Jewish, and I think two of us will." When asked why she thinks this sense of responsibility largely falls on her shoulders, Ruth suggests:

> I think that the responsibility that my mother felt has been ingrained in me, not so much my brother. You know, boys grow up to be like their fathers, girls grow up to be like their mothers. I think that I have a lot of that. It's just something I've always taken more seriously than my siblings for whatever reason.

Whether or not the split between the genders fully explains the role that Ruth plays in her family, undertaking the battle to "never forget" has become her lifelong journey. Alongside this responsibility, the issues of respect, the "strength" of her present Jewish identity, the past murder of her family members, and the desire to raise Jewish children in the future all blend into one: "I feel like that would be disrespectful and not continuing the importance and the strength of how I identify, and how much of my family was killed, and so many of those issues that

CHAPTER EIGHT

to me create a really strong force and desire to have a Jewish family." One sentence summarizes one ongoing, collective narrative.

Understandably, Ruth fears that "there is a lot of forgetting that is about to go on," feeling that history, like pride, is a fragile, vulnerable entity. What will happen when her children can no longer "touch" a survivor (or be touched by one)? Will they continue to "know" their collective trauma, to feel the complicated combination of shame, pride, and fear that she experiences? Is grappling with a constant threat of annihilation synonymous with maintaining a Jewish identity? Or can her children identify themselves as Jews without the torment of regular confrontations with the past? In attempting to describe her grandfather's Holocaust stories, Ruth reveals:

> I mean, I lost track of some of them, I was so young... it's like, what do you know when you're like five years old? I remember him sitting me down on his lap and trying to tell me these things and I had a) no interest, and b) no patience. I wanted to go run around and do whatever... so I felt very cheated later after he died because so many things that he wanted to share that aren't there anymore.

Ruth's words illustrate that the obstruction of history is a very real and omnipresent fear, one that Ruth has tackled head on, but that began first and foremost in her own personal experience. Having had "a) no interest, and b) no patience," a five-year-old Ruth turned away from her grandfather's lap, causing the details of his stories to disappear from her conscious memory. On some level, it seems Ruth hopes that her efforts to "never forget" will not only ensure the survival of Holocaust history at large, but might also reinstate her grandfather's lost tales, resurfacing and reestablishing the truths of his-story. Concretely, Ruth goes a step further in her efforts to transmit a disappearing history; below she describes a murdered relative, a ghost, who has accompanied the family narrative from past to present, and will be carried into the future:

> R: My grandfather's sister, who I obviously never met, but whenever I think about her... I guess probably because I identify... she was 12 and she was killed right away and that breaks my heart.

N: Why do you think it's her?
R: I think because she's someone specific; she was a young female. I've heard him talk about her. She was his baby sister. And his mother, who he described as the best woman ever... and I'm sure his sister was her little angel.
N: What was her name?
R: Toni.
N: Do you think you'll name children after...?
R: Yeah.

Ruth feels personally and intimately connected to her grandfather's murdered sister, clinging to a fantasy of the person and maintaining a relationship to her name. The Holocaust therefore attains a present-day feel, and the murder of Toni carries the weight of someone Ruth knew well in present time. Thus, every anti-Semitic individual, every questioning 13-year-old, every ignorant or fearful or hateful person produces a threat; however, this is not a threat that history *might* at any moment reappear, but rather a realization that history *does* at every moment reappear. After all, a sense of safety, acceptance, and equality (all internal and external experiences) have not yet been achieved. Furthermore, Ruth describes one of her recent conversations about whether or not she should "hate all Germans," who themselves believed, "we hate these Jews; we want to kill them":

> I don't feel hopeless. I do feel that there is a lot of anti-Semitism still. Actually, I had a conversation last week about "Do I hate all Germans? Should we hate all Germans?" Well, I mean, the obvious answer is kind of like, not all Germans did this and that's a little bit of a ridiculous stance to take, but I was in Germany when I was abroad for a weekend and I will tell you I felt very uncomfortable. Even hearing the language made me uncomfortable. I can't imagine what it would do to my grandparents. And I think even within the United States... even within D.C., or wherever it is, and... we live in a largely Jewish... at least a largely Jewishly-aware city, and I still think there's a level there that people don't even talk about... the same that there's racism against

blacks that people don't talk about. Maybe they talk about it more, I don't know. When I had this conversation about "Should we hate all Germans?" with someone, what I said was, "Look at those people's grandparents, right? Cause it's the same third generation. So they grew up like, 'We hate these Jews; we want to kill them.' Those are their grandparents. Maybe they really disagree, but a lot of them... that's kind of what they grew up with, and that's scary." And to say that these people are so far different from their grandparents I think is a leap of faith that I don't know if I'm personally comfortable taking. I think that that's like a jump... that's a big jump... Putting a lot of faith in people that I don't know if I have.

Ruth speaks to an ongoing sense of fear and insecurity that she carries, as the Germans of Nazi Germany and contemporary Germany blend into inseparable entities; after all, she likewise reveals the ways in which third-generation Holocaust survivors, deeply impacted by their traumatic history, are intertwined with their ancestors' experiences. She wonders to what extent "faith in people" will allow her to consider "that these people are so far different from their grandparents," ultimately deciding that "that's a big jump." When past and present collide, therefore, the leap towards something "so far different" is immense. Ruth's question about hating "all" Germans is provoked by Nazi Germany, although it is asked within the context of a "Jewishly-aware" city. As she tackles some difficult questions related to projection and introjection—they hate us so we should hate them—her collective, historically-laden fear, shame, and pride are tangible. Towards the end of her interview, I asked Ruth about her mother's choice of the mental health profession:

> No, I never asked her how she really got interested. I think she probably needed a way to kind of figure out what was going on with them and how that related to her, because it's a real big burden to bear even if you understand it. She still gets upset with her mother all the time, with someone who you can honestly understand what's going on, but understanding and feeling are two different things.

"...but understanding and feeling are two different things," Ruth suggests, shedding light on her own separation between what she knows and what she experiences. While she knows that Jewish pride is a fundamental element of her self-esteem, she cannot help but feel occasional fear, shame, and embarrassment about her history. Although she understands that she was born generations after the Holocaust, she oftentimes experiences historical dynamics unfolding in the present. Finally, while she knows that nothing can undo her painful past, she feels that grappling with it might lessen the blow of the traumatic event. Thus, Ruth concludes, "...it's a real big burden to bear even if you understand it," highlighting the ultimate, unavoidable meeting between knowledge and emotion.

CHAPTER 9: MIRIAM

M: I also have kind of a rebellious side. I've gotten a lot of emotional satisfaction out of feeling... sort of rebuffing what I'm supposed to be. Another interesting piece... my first love was this Slovak guy from Eastern Europe who was Christian... wore a cross around his neck... and it was like years of devastating... I didn't date him for years, but... not Jewish, he was from Eastern Europe, from Slovakia. I went to visit him once with his grandmother and like, they had, like, chicken soup with matzo balls but they were long and not round, and there were like, donuts with jelly on the side and... I was very, very pulled to him... like, oh my God, his grandmother was a collaborator with the Germans. And he'd tell me stuff and anyway... I played out a lot of stuff around a lot of rebelliousness. Also, I think I felt close to him. In some ways there was a lot of cultural difference... but I think I also felt really comfortable with him. There was something comforting for me with him. He was from Eastern Europe and anyways there was a lot of kind of intrigue...
N: How was that for you, the religious differences, background differences... all the things that came to mind?
M: It felt really wrenching. I think for a while he didn't tell his family that I was Jewish. He had an uncle who was a priest, and thought he would be disapproving... like, took me to see the area that used to be the Jewish part of town... it was clearly abandoned. Told me the Germans had taken over his grandfather's house and the backyard and stuff and I really had this sense of like... it was awful, I felt like I was in bed with a collaborator and it was killing my grandmother, and my mom was extremely opposed to it; said it wasn't going to be good for me, that I would have... you know, there was a lot of deterrence. I felt really fragmented. I didn't know how

my Jewish self was going to be. It was also really interesting and intriguing to be like in a church in Slovakia and Kristallnacht was there. It was also exciting… I definitely played it out like constantly.

"I've gotten a lot of emotional satisfaction out of feeling… sort of rebuffing what I'm supposed to be," says 29-year-old Miriam, a half-Israeli, half-American, third generation descendant of the Holocaust. Her tale of her "first love" powerfully captures how history comes alive in her present-day existence. "I was very, very pulled to him," she reflects, and the meeting of a Jewish descendant of a Holocaust survivor and a Christian descendant of Slovak "collaborators" is saturated with images linked to past and present. Miriam conveys the "comforting" but also "wrenching" effects of this bond; after all, the connection they shared was established three-quarters of a century ago, under circumstances diametrically opposed to the present. Through her "rebellious" nature, Miriam blurs the boundaries between love and hate, rebelliousness and allegiance, owned and disowned identity. While she feels she is "rebuffing" who she is "supposed to be"—referring to herself as divided from her ancestors—it is precisely in this "rebuffing" that Miriam summons her roots. In a sense, she "plays out" an existence entrenched in repetition and reenactment: finding herself in a "comforting," yet "wrenching" dynamic, struggling to grasp and loosen the tie of history. To do so, she reenters her ancestors' world, "in bed with a collaborator," "killing" her grandmother, feeling "fragmented," "intrigued," and fused with the experience of the Holocaust.

Miriam goes on to verbalize feeling "tortured" and "haunted" by this experience years later:

> M: He was basically… I had come back and he was finishing up another year and I was graduating from college and trying to figure out what to do with myself. And he was really ready to move out to Chicago. I was totally tortured and I just thought, well, what kind of job is he gonna get and am I going to have to move out to Slovakia? What do I do? And the religion thing was huge, and I didn't know what to do, and so I broke up with him… but then I really felt haunted by it for like

> years later. We still write each other cards in the mail. He's been with the same woman for... I don't feel like it's processed... often when I talk about it I'll start crying. I felt like he was this ghost that was like haunting me for years and I really regretted breaking up with him.
> N: Yeah, in a way he represented so much more... he was himself, but he was also...
> M: Right. He was this whole different world, he was also... I was playing out everything—relationships, power... it was extremely exciting for me.

By "playing out everything—relationships, power..." Miriam and her "first love" engaged in an enactment of their shared history, both attempting to master something unknowable and inexplicable. As she took on the more powerful role and ended the relationship, Miriam instantaneously challenged the course of history in the present (in her exertion of power), but also left history untouched (in that history can be forever replayed but not reversed). Furthermore, the impact of terminating this connection was devastating for her, as Miriam experienced a sense of loss and distance from this man, and from the history that bound them together. She states, "I felt like he was this ghost that was like haunting me for years..." That is, with the termination of the concrete, the bond evolved into an elusive, ever-present awareness of all that was lost. While this man seems to have entered a new relationship, Miriam is left feeling that the entire experience remains unprocessed, and that she might "start crying" whenever she speaks of it. Therefore, her statement "it was extremely exciting for me" speaks to the exhilarating revival of history and all of its accompanying emotions and dynamics. In the ensuing discussion of Miriam's subsequent decision to date only Jews, Miriam reveals:

> M: I think it felt better to me. I think for a long time it really felt like... maybe as I've gotten older and I've gotten closer to sort of feeling like wanting to get married or something like that it just felt better... but I think for a long time I think "Jewish" meant being married with a white picket fence and stuck and boring and suburbia...

acquiescing and not being an individual... which makes sense in my family... I tend to be attracted to people that have some good amount of push and pull with religion.
N: Do you envision raising your kids Jewish?
M: Yeah, although when I think about what kind of stories I'm going to tell them, I don't know very many...
N: Well, you have your own stories.
M: Right, I have my own stories.

In Miriam's depiction, "Jewish" seems to stand for "free of conflict," lacking a "push and pull with religion" and also with history. She explains, "...'Jewish' meant being married with a white picket fence and stuck and boring and suburbia... acquiescing and not being an individual..." That is, Miriam's definition of the word "Jewish" means to escape "being an individual," and falling into a preformed mold that might prevent her from asserting control, expressing her individuality, and developing a unique sense of self. Interestingly, the image of the "white picket fence" serves as an American symbol of the ideal middle-class suburban life, with a family, 2.5 children, sizeable house, and serene existence. Unsurprisingly, Miriam feels impelled to escape this standard, as it does not capture her individual or collective identity. As she explicitly states in the opening of her interview, "My grandparents had accents and I was very convinced that was the normal course of things, although it also made me feel different than my American Jewish peers. I just didn't quite identify with American Judaism." In her rebellion from "American Judaism," Miriam simultaneously searches for her roots. In retrospect, my comment "Well, you have your own stories" seems to address the fact that whether or not she knows her ancestor's specific tales, she quite evidently and concretely merges with her history, discovering parts of herself along the way. Ironically though perhaps not surprisingly, Miriam later discusses her grandmother's "secretive" nature, and reveals a striking parallel between her grandmother and herself, stating in passing, "She was in love with a non-Jew and you know there was all this... she's just very, very secretive." This intergenerational repetition of patterns reveals Miriam's ever-present connection with history, even in her disconnect from the details.

CHAPTER NINE

Binging on History

Miriam contextualizes the fact that she does not "know" very many stories through a description of her mother's lifelong accumulation of "all" the stories:

> I think she feels it's her responsibility of the second generation to like have all the information. She must have sensed a lot of the sadness of her parents having lost that old world, and their approach, I think, was try to forget it, and hers was to try to recover it and contain it. I'm sure she and I in very different ways have tried to find ways to master and try to make sense of a lot of pain and disruption, and that was her way of doing it.

Miriam's insight regarding her attempts to "master" and "make sense of a lot of pain and disruption" is compelling; while her grandparents attempted to "forget" their sadness and her mother worked hard to "recover it and contain it," Miriam is left with a determination to not "acquiesce" to either pattern. Thus, she chooses not to take in the stories, yet to maintain connection to her history in her own way. Miriam continues:

> M: I feel like I… I think it's probably typical… my mother like wants to be… sees herself as the memory receptacle. She's constantly asking extremely detailed questions to my grandmother and my great aunts and uncle about, like, before the war and during the war. She wants the details and the history and you know… at this point she has more of it than my grandmother does because my grandmother kind of gets confused… or she'll remind my grandmother what was in her house, or you know… or she'll like trace… she's obsessed. The first thing she does is finds out a last name and tries to trace like family lineage in Eastern Europe and she… like, she can be diagnosed with PTSD. She's extremely fearful. There's always impending disaster. She's very good in crisis.
> N: Can you give an example of that fear… how that impacts her?

M: My father has commuted to Chicago for the last five years and she won't sleep in bed without him, she sleeps on the couch, and has like a scissor under her cushion and the alarm is on and she will often... whenever I go out somewhere she'll tell me to take my ID with me and I'll ask her why, and she's like, "In case you die they can identify the body." She's just overprotective throughout and just has issues... she's definitely gotten better. You can just see she has the worst-case scenario... she's highly anxious, she's really reactive... she probably has survivor skills. She's obese, she has diabetes; she cannot take care of herself. She spends a lot of time obsessing about my grandmother. I guess that's another reason why my grandmother is alive... with the case of survivors, they can't let themselves go because they're worried that if they do die it will destroy their children. And my mother's like really concerned about keeping her alive even though she's in a wheelchair and catheterized and quite unhappy a lot of the time.

Miriam's mother serves as the "memory receptacle" for her family, growing increasingly obese with all that she takes in. That is, in order to "master" her history, she is impelled to "recover and contain" all of the historical pain, literally and figuratively stuffing herself full. As Miriam describes, "she's like a *repository* for all this terrible stuff." On the one hand, therefore, her mother's obesity symbolizes her ancestors' starvation; on the other hand, Miriam's mother is literally overextended by the burden of the past. She cannot possibly "take care of herself," because she is far too busy "obsessing" about Miriam's grandmother, spending an entire lifetime "keeping her alive." The transmission of anxiety, distrust, and fear are evident in Miriam's concrete examples of her mother sleeping with scissors under her cushion and demanding that Miriam carry an ID so that her dead body might be identified. Furthermore, as Miriam states, "she can be diagnosed with PTSD. She's extremely fearful. There's always impending disaster. She's very good in crisis." That is, traumatized by her ancestors' experiences, Miriam's mother "can be diagnosed with PTSD," as though she survived the experience herself.

CHAPTER NINE

Attempting to Restrict the Past

Miriam describes the ways in which she disconnects from her mother's stories, and more generally establishes boundaries between her mother and herself:

> M: I mean, she usually doesn't get totally through a story. I mean, she'll start to tell me something and I'll kind of try to listen because like she's trying to tell me something and part of me thinks I'd want to know some this stuff in the future. And about two or three sentences later I haven't heard a word she's saying. We're somewhere in the middle of like Poland or Russia, and she'll talk for a while and I'm not listening but I'm kind of nodding, and then at some point I'm just like, I can't hear anymore. Thanks, I'm done.
>
> N: Is that generally kind of your reaction to her? Or mostly just on that topic?
>
> M: No, she and I also clash and I find her overwhelming in general, and I think that's a good classification of things. But, no, I often find her kind of boundary-bending or there's stuff kind of spilling over into our world or... I think when I was younger for a long time I felt like... or you know, the beginning stages of therapy... that I had no idea who, or what, were my emotions and what were anyone else's... I think my father also had a traumatic childhood and I was depressed and I didn't really have a sense of what it was. I didn't think it was mine, I think... I mean it was mine, you know, carrying around a lot of their stuff. So I think I got... I tried to create boundaries.

As the boundaries are blurred and her mother's experience begins "spilling over" into Miriam's world, Miriam successfully blocks out the stimuli. "I'll kind of try to listen because like she's trying to tell me something and part of me thinks I'd want to know some this stuff in the future. And about two or three sentences later I haven't heard a word she's saying," she explains. Ultimately, she is left with the feeling, "I can't hear anymore. Thanks, I'm done." Having been completely overwhelmed by her grandmother's past experience as well as her mother's reaction to history, Miriam understands that much of what she is filled with is "a lot of their stuff." She perceptively states, "I had no idea who, or what, were my emotions and what were anyone else's." That is, she had no idea whose emotions she was carrying or who she suddenly embodied. She did, however, sense, "I didn't think it was mine," and protectively attempted to set boundaries in place.

In separating herself from her mother and from historical narrative, Miriam does not become emotionless or unaware. Instead, her distance from the familial enmeshment and chaos allows her to more fully explore and understand her experience. The importance of her successfully doing so can be seen in her discussion of "crazy-making" experiences with her mother. That is, Miriam seems to be fighting not only for individuality, but also for her sanity:

> Something just happened to me the other day and it's… oh, I got home and she was cooking and I said, "Is dinner going to be soon? I'm hungry and I'm wondering if I should have a snack or not." And she said, "No, it won't be for a while," which to me means hours. So I had a larger snack. Fifteen minutes later my dad is home and she said, "Whenever you guys want to eat" and my dad said, "I'm hungry" and I said, "Didn't you say dinner would be in a while?" and she denied the two of us having had that exchange. Later I said, "You know, if you forgot or changed your mind or made a mistake, it's not a big deal. But when you deny the exchange happened, it makes me so confused about reality. It makes me feel like I'm crazy." She just can't… she's like, "Why do you get so angry?" You know. There's just no way of talking to her most of the time. We often get into a clash which will be about something and then we just let it drop and come back together and we're fine… instead of talking it out. I don't know.

Miriam attempts to explain "…when you deny the exchange happened, it makes me so confused about reality. It makes me feel like I'm crazy." That is, in addition to not knowing which thought or emotion

CHAPTER NINE

belongs to her, Miriam also cannot trust the events that unfold in her everyday life. She winds up feeling "so confused" about reality, as she cannot distinguish true from false, hers from theirs, reality from fantasy. While she confronts her mother about the impact of altogether denying a real exchange, it seems that there is often "no way of talking," no true communication, between mother and daughter. The lack of a shared language, therefore, sheds further light on Miriam's desire not to know her family's stories, or to actively seek out past trauma; after all, the present is already brimming with the trauma of the past, and is in and of itself overwhelming. Along these lines, Miriam explains her conscious effort not to engulf herself in Holocaust-related films or books:

> I feel like there is this place in me that can just be totally bottomed out and I know where it is and have done enough of it and I'm just not interested... I feel like it floods me or I get flooded. Like, I don't understand what purpose it has for me. Like, as an educational tool... the same questions as my mother's stories. Like, do I need any more details? Like, I certainly don't know very much about it... Like, I feel like the acquisition of that information just feels like an emotional overload. I don't know what purpose it has for me. I don't know how to translate the "Never forget" message... do I think it's important? Do I identify with the AJWF global social justice movement approach? But no, I... I don't know... I don't want to be inundated with it. I want it to be useful to me. I'm not using it in a generative way. I don't know... maybe it'll change...

In an effort to not be "totally bottomed out" but rather make it "useful" for herself, Miriam attempts to acquire historical information in moderation. She adds, "I find my way of dealing with it is to download articles or something." That is, "articles" related to her Holocaust history seem to provide an accessible amount of information, which serve a "purpose" and remain a "generative" tool. Indeed, it seems Miriam's established boundaries between herself and her history are firm. However, in a brief discussion about her father's lineage, Miriam reveals a much more extensive curiosity and connection to his experiences of loss and grief. When asked what might have drawn her more to her paternal history, Miriam suggests, "Maybe I was trying to piece together my dad more. He could be very calm but then some sort of invisible wire will trip him. You know, it was really very clear what was going on with my mom…" Despite her clashes with her mother, Miriam innately understands and identifies with her mother's experiences. Furthermore, regardless of her established boundaries or desire for distance, Miriam maintains an instinctive closeness to, and knowledge of, her Holocaust history. With or without the details, the past is inescapably a part of her.

Maintaining Weight and Substance

M: I went to a nutritionist senior year of high school and I got myself to a therapist my sophomore year of college and I think I constantly negotiated issues around like having a very loving family, it's very enmeshed, it's very sad in some ways—being a part of the family means sort of being sad and depressed and having my mother in particular sort of make these clinical, global statements about the family.
N: "Everyone's depressed? Everyone's sad?"
M: Right, and if my sister's not… it's strange, how did that kind of emerge? I mean, my sister also has her own anxieties. The apple doesn't fall far from the tree. So, I think it's individuating and being not severely depressed, but all those things that come with fears of being abandoned.
N: How did you get yourself to a nutritionist?
M: I had some kind of weird eating habits in high school. It wasn't awful but it was uncomfortable and I think I instinctively have like, "something's wrong and I'm gonna take care of it" approach.
N: So you were eating a lot or you were constricting?
M: Both. I sort of remember I wasn't eating until I got home from school, and I was binge eating and tried to make myself throw up a few times and I just couldn't. I was really eating a ton of food. It felt awful.

CHAPTER NINE

Describing how she found her way to a nutritionist and a therapist—and later, into the mental health profession—Miriam reveals some of the insights she acquired along the way. For example, "Being a part of the family means sort of being sad and depressed and having my mother in particular sort of make these clinical, global statements about the family." A number of questions arise from this exploration: how much of herself does Miriam have to sacrifice in order to remain an accepted member of the family? Will she be able to balance "individuating and not being severely depressed" with her "fears of being abandoned"? Or will she continue to contain other people's emotions and experiences, regardless of her attempts to establish distance and boundaries? Miriam reveals the difficulty of truly separating, as fears of being "alone" ultimately carry her back to her family:

> There was some point in grad school where it felt very clear to me I was done being depressed, and all of a sudden I was extremely anxious and kind of panic attack-y. And occasionally, in the last five years, there have been times when I'm really afraid I'm gonna get really, really depressed and that just hasn't happened. I think I'm now less anxious than I was in the first sort of kind of flip. I don't think it's uncommon that those mix together. Not recently but I certainly like… when I was in graduate school in the middle of the night there was this sudden like, "I'm alone" and worried about my parents dying and constantly visualizing…

In acknowledging that she was "done being depressed" and finding herself feeling "less anxious" than before, Miriam separates herself from her family. Moments later, however, she reveals an arising fear of her "parents dying." On some level, it seems that separating and finding herself to not be anxious, or to not be depressed, is a dangerous pursuit; one that might even kill off her parents. It is no wonder, therefore, that statements like "Everyone's depressed" and "Everyone's sad" provide a sense of safety for Miriam and her mother. After all, "clinical, global statements about the family" are by definition "global," such that Miriam will not have to carry them on her own. Thus, Miriam responds to a question about depression with, "No... I don't feel depressed. I think my baseline might be a little lower..." Her "baseline" is indeed "lower," because if it were higher she might find herself "alone."

Miriam concludes her interview by questioning her choice of social work as her profession and doubting her ability to feel "empathetic" towards others:

> Part of me also wonders what kind of... do I want to hear about other people's problems, or is this about my own stories? Like, this doesn't have to be my role... I can do something else, I can think about the world. I can think about social structures. I don't have to exist in this murky, complicated vortex of feelings with superposed structures that make your life complicated. People ... They're interesting... I think sometimes the experience of having patients is... they can be different enough from me that it doesn't really trigger feelings of being haunted by someone else's stuff. Sometimes I feel like my empathetic response has been turned off too much. I don't think it has... I just was like way too sensitive... I just really had to kind of control it.

While Miriam hopes to achieve some "mastery" and "control" over her feelings, believing she was "way too sensitive" in the past, she has thus far been unable to separate from the "murky, complicated vortex of feelings" that dominates her day-to-day life. Hopefully, she will never completely separate from this type of "existence." After all, while she claims, "this doesn't have to be my role," she finds herself pulled towards helping "people" and more fully understanding herself. Thus, the question, "do I want to hear about other people's problems, or is this about my own stories?" seems superfluous. It is through her own stories and experiences that she will better understand, tolerate, and feel empathy for "other people's problems."

CHAPTER 10: MALKA

> There's something about women being the carriers of the stories. Women are the carriers of history. I think there are some things she told me that she would never even tell my dad. I think even my maternal grandmother tells me things that she doesn't tell anybody else either. There's something about being a granddaughter… there's something about being a woman. One woman will tell… I think men… I don't think my grandfather would have ever told me anything. He was a very quiet and sweet man. I don't know if that was ever something that was even talked about at all. According to my dad, it was simply not talked about at home. It was just known and it was not spoken of, but I think she thought it was something that was important for me to know her story. You know, I think my brothers got snippets, again, packaged in my presence, you know like, "And this is why you should do things, because these things can happen." But, I think there was something different about telling me versus telling them. There's something very maternal about having that. It's like an emotional burden that women carry and I don't know if men can carry it or if men would share that. I think that she knew that in telling me it would be passed on; and telling me, it's something that's kept sacred.

"Women are the carriers of history," says 29-year-old Malka, understanding that "there's something about being a granddaughter" that unites her with a lineage of stories and storytellers. She is a link in an ongoing chain of women who serve as imparters of all that was lost, and all that remains, of the Holocaust. The image of women bonding in Anita Diamant's (1997) fictional novel *The Red Tent*, sharing tales and experiences within a community of women, hovers nearby throughout our discussion. "It was just known and it was not spoken of," she says, with resolve to do things differently. Malka recounts her grandparents' escape and survival of the Holocaust: while her 18-year-old grandfather chose to separate from his family and trek from Poland to Russia by foot, her 14-year-old grandmother was ordered by her parents "don't come home" from summer camp, and was likewise the family's sole survivor. Herself half-Israeli, half-American, and living in the U.S., Malka's identity comprises various splits: Israeli versus American, survivor versus escaper, the bearer of knowledge and language within a family of silence and disownment. Malka believes, "There's something very maternal about having that. It's like an emotional burden that women carry and I don't know if men can carry it or if men would share that." Throughout her interview, Malka quite clearly depicts the ways in which she holds, nourishes, and fosters the "emotional burden" that is her history, much like a mother sustains her baby. "I think that she knew that in telling me it would be passed on; and telling me, it's something that's kept sacred." Malka, the third generation keeper of her "sacred" family record, is at once the inheritor, possessor, and imparter of history. Malka goes on:

> So it's passed on through the women. I don't think that men necessarily share these things in the same way. I don't think they have the hearts to hearts; they don't have the conversation; it's simply not in their ... it's not how they're socialized. They bury their feelings, they bury their traumas; they deal with it, they suck it up and they move on... despite the emotional ramifications that come thereafter, but they don't deal with it. They don't talk about it... whereas women, we do—we talk, we cope, we rely on each other, we talk about things with our family. My dad, you know, not so much. Only again, later in life and only to me... doesn't talk to my brothers about these things either... doesn't talk to my brothers about how hard it was to lose his mom... doesn't talk to my brothers about how hard it is for him to be alone now and how it ... You know, the loss of his mom, the loss of his whole family, and what that means to him.

"I don't think they have the hearts to hearts" says Malka, knowing men to turn away from emotional connection and exploration, choosing instead to "deal" with their traumas by curbing them and focusing elsewhere: "They bury their feelings, they bury their traumas," she says, "...despite the emotional ramifications that come thereafter." Her word choice referring to the way men "suck it up" is interesting, given that the slang expression suggests a tendency to deal with something difficult or unpleasant by shutting it out; in another sense, however, to "suck it up" means to take in, and absorb, the material. Thus, even in burying their feelings, or perhaps especially in burying their feelings, the emotions are sucked in, and soaked up. Whether or not this gender split—women "cope" and men "bury" their traumas—is a clear-cut differentiation beyond Malka's experience, she speaks to the division between those who sustain curiosity about themselves and their history, and those who choose not to know. In a later discussion of her mother, Malka reveals, "My mom didn't really talk about it. To her, she was Israeli, and that was all there is to know." In other words, her mother's sense of self was entirely fabricated by the fragments of identity she selected for herself. After all, as Malka explains, her maternal, "Israeli" lineage is intimately intertwined with the Holocaust and survivors:

> ...My mom's family is sixth generation Israeli. They've been there for a very long time, and my grandmother actually grew up on the beaches of Tel Aviv, like where all the hotels are now—that's where she lives. Her family was helping smuggle in survivors. Her family was bringing them in and housing them and hiding them because they lived right on the beach.

Whether female or male, resistance to talking about "what that means" is widespread, and carries "emotional ramifications that come thereafter"—way after, for generations to come.

"There's Simply No One"

> M: Yeah, I don't know. My dad, he never talked to me about it... snippets here and there, but it was never something that was... the fact that I only learned about a lot of these things when I was in my mid-20s, I mean, kind

of tells about how little I knew growing up. I knew where they were from. I knew that they had lost their family. I knew basics... they went to Russia... I didn't even know the real story of how she got there. I didn't know... she didn't even tell me like, how did she even deal with being there? Her family was not that far and she had no idea where they were. You know, how do you even deal with that as a teenager? I can't even fathom. I can't fathom losing my parents now, how do you deal with that at 14? I didn't even get the story from my grandfather because he passed away when I was young. How do you make a decision when you're 18 years old to just pack up and leave? Like, how do you do that? How do you say, "I'm going to save myself"? I don't know.
N: It is completely unfathomable.
M: It is unfathomable. You know, like God forbid we ever know something like that, but like, how do you make those decisions? How do you say like: "I don't care if you don't believe me anymore, I'm not sticking around to see how this ends?" I don't know. And there's something that saddens me so much about the fact that I don't know, that that part of us is lost, and because there's no other family it's never going to be known.

Malka's questions wrestle with *how* her grandparents were able to survive their past experiences: "... how did she even deal with being there? ... how do you even deal with that as a teenager? ... How do you make a decision when you're 18 years old to just pack up and leave? ... how do you do that? How do you say 'I'm going to save myself'?" Indeed, the decisions they made, the lifesaving determination that impelled them, and their capacity to persevere is unfathomable. Within the established boundaries of language and silence, Malka never found the opportunity to verbalize these questions to her grandparents. Perhaps she formulated her questions in depth, considered posing them at some point, or even approached them with curiosity. However, the time was never right because the message was clear: listen to what I choose to tell you and do not press for further information. Alongside her history, therefore, Malka's unanswered questions remain. Her sense of not

CHAPTER TEN

knowing the full truth about her family, and herself, is ever-present: "And there's something that saddens me so much about the fact that I don't know, that that part of us is lost, and because there's no other family it's never going to be known."

Malka continues to dwell on the concrete fact that "There's no one" alive anymore to shed light on the past:

> It's not like there are secret cousins that could be living somewhere that like, "Oh, maybe they know." It's just gone. That whole generation, even my grandmother's aunt, didn't have any children. I mean, there's nobody. There's nobody at all. There's not someone random, like a descendant of someone that can figure out how to piecemeal it together. There's no one. That to me is… the kind of sadness and grief and trauma that's carried on is that there's simply no one. There's no one to carry on the legacy. There's no one to even know it happened. And I think the past year or so is what my dad's really been trying to deal with and struggle with is this… lack. It's just gone.

Malka reiterates, "It's just gone … there's nobody. There's nobody at all. There's not someone random, like a descendant of someone that can figure out how to piecemeal it together. There's no one." She repeats this thought time and again, emphasizing and simultaneously contemplating the meaning of her words. How can there be no one? What happens if not a single person can explain or at least assemble some missing pieces of her history? Will she forever feel confused by and futilely compelled to understand—like "pieces" of a "meal" that will never fully satisfy her? As she insightfully explains, it is precisely in not knowing, in the utter "lack" of her history, that trauma is transmitted: "…the kind of sadness and grief and trauma that's carried on is that there's simply no one." In this way, Malka continues to carry the "emotional burden" of her history because there is "no one" to fill the emptiness within her. Furthermore, Malka's comment that "God forbid we ever know something like that" suggests that knowledge of the event occurs only through the experience itself. That is, even answers and stories will fail to clarify the unknowable. As Malka later states in conversation about her grandmother:

"I only started getting these little snippets of stories as she was kind of preparing for her departure from this world. Like, 'There are things I need to tell you. I didn't tell you these things before; this is what you need to know.'" These "snippets," however, cannot fill the void of history.

Thus, Malka is left with endless questions, wondering how her grandparents were able to persevere. What impelled them to maintain strength? How did they go on? What was it like? Where did they turn? How did they feel? Malka believes she will be unable to fully understand herself, and her place within the context of her ancestors, as long as she remains cut off from the details of her past. Deep down, however, it seems that Malka holds the answers to some of her questions, without having ever heard them from another family member. That is, the answers lie within herself:

> But there were no stories. There was no talk about it at all, and that part of our history was very much lost in our family, I think. We don't even have a proper telling of what happened because they were so traumatized and so alone that they just wanted to move on. They in many ways gave up their Judaism, they in many ways... they had ham in the house... and were not very observant, and I mean, they never really were, but it was something that was so... I mean, my last name is now Dan. My last name wasn't Dan; my last name was Davidson. My dad changed it. You know, very much don't want to deal with your Jewish identity. That was something only bad things came from. While they were clearly Zionists and believed in the state of Israel, there was something that separated being Israeli and being a *shtetl*[1] Jew, and those two things are different and they would be different and we will make it different. So that kind of cutoff between the past and what is the future, and how we are going to make that future, was very evident because that was just not spoken about.

---

1 The Yiddish word "shtetl" is derived from the German word "Stadt," town. "Shtetl" often refers to a town with a large Jewish population in pre-Holocaust Europe.

CHAPTER TEN

The apparent disconnect between the truths of the past and desire for the future is a powerful one. Speaking to the well-recognized, post-Holocaust contradiction between the strong, independent Israeli Jew, and the weak, powerless *shtetl* Jew of Eastern Europe, Malka reveals her family's belief that "…those two things are different and they would be different and we will make it different." In a sense, her family, along with an entire (young) nation of Israelis sculpting an identity immediately following the Holocaust, maintains that the past is not the past if one chooses to avoid it. Thus, she says, our future "would be different" because "we will make it different." The word *Sabra*, meaning an Israeli-born Jew, is derived from the Hebrew name for the prickly pear cactus "tzabar." The reference is to a resilient, thorny plant with a thick external coat and a softer interior; that is, rough on the outside, but sensitive on the inside. The stereotypical distinction between masculine and feminine once again arises in this label, as does the split between one's external and internal self. However, the modern, post-Holocaust Israeli Jew might in many ways be a new type of Jew, but simultaneously remains the same old Jew with a new shell: hardened over time. Furthermore, while the image of the strong and forceful Israeli Jew seeks to eliminate the weak, fragile, and passive representation of the European *shtetl* Jew, the two remain intimately intertwined. Malka therefore says "we will make it different" instead of "it is different," because Davidson turned into Dan only after a deliberate attempt to cut out the middle. One name clearly defines the other, just like "strong" elucidates the meaning of "weak," "masculine" relates to "feminine," and "there were no stories" gives greater meaning to an hour and a half interview.

"Such a Big Deal"

Feeling cut off from her history, Malka goes on to reveal the tangible roots of this disconnect:

> M: My mom didn't really talk about it. To her, she was Israeli and that was all there is to know. And again, I think it's a part of that "We're Israeli and that's who we are." Everything that came before us before that was before that; this is our new identity.
> N: It's so interesting, trying to start anew and believing

that the past won't be carried on within…

M: So many of our family friends who are Israeli changed their last names. It's all kind of shortened; it's easier to say; no longer Jewish sounding. Davidson to Dan—I mean, could you be any shorter? You could've just said "D." Very much breaking away from that past, breaking away from that part of their identity. And while it's so important for them to have us to be Jewish, it's to be Jewish in a certain way.

In her mother's assigning a single, new label for her identity—"Israeli"—or her father's shortening his name from "Davidson" to "Dan," the history of Malka's family is literally abridged. Past attempts to wipe the slate clean, however, leave Malka with a sense of lack and ignite her quest for something more. Her sense of personal responsibility to carry the past, present, and future, for herself and for her entire family, is evident. "There's something very maternal about having that," she says, because for Malka, her history has become like her baby: she cannot go back in time, undo, or escape the connection to her past; and on most days, she would not want to. Instead, she will forever uphold it, feed it, and convey its meaning to future generations, doing everything in her power to keep it alive. After all, who else would care for this child? "There's simply no one" that is willing to help carry the load. Not surprisingly, in discussing potential baby names for her future children, Malka states, "Mind you, my ovaries are totally not ready for any of the babies at all, but if one more person tells me they're pregnant, I'm gonna lose my mind." Her envy of others' pregnancies is understandable, given that there is no room for "any of the babies" in her life so long as baby history is at the forefront, demanding attention and consideration.

Along similar lines, Malka's father struggles to incorporate his children in his definition of the word "family" and in his sense of place in the world. How can others exist when history and all of its figures overpower the present? What is the place of his descendants, if connection to his ancestors has been disavowed? Malka describes her father's mentality following the death of his mother:

> But I think it was not just loss of a mother; it was loss of the family. Like, "I'm an orphan. I have no one. I have no

CHAPTER TEN

family. There's no one to help me with this. There's no one to help me take care of anything. I'm by myself." And I was like, "Dad, you have us." He was like, "It's just not the same. Of course, I have you. Of course you're my... but it's just different."

Sadly, Malka's father feels that "I have no one. I have no family," even in the midst of a conversation with his daughter. Indeed, as he explains, "It's just not the same"; after all, in his mind, his offspring are detached from their predecessors, precisely because he had wanted it so. Yet, as he finds himself alone, seemingly the last survivor of a vanishing history, he feels "There's no one to help me take care of anything. I'm by myself." Thus, his attempts to wipe out his past seem to have frozen his grief in time. Malka insightfully captures this phenomenon:

> I was sensitive enough to know she'll share with me what she wants when she wants to because otherwise it wouldn't be such a big deal. It was just this unspoken-of thing that hung over my dad and his parents... it was just this like unspoken-of, constant grief that was there. And so I would never... I would ask once in a while but like... it's interesting. I actually look like my grandmother's mother... like, frighteningly so. And so she has this one picture of her parents—that's the only picture she has—and we now have it. She doesn't have any pictures of her little brother. There was just so much that was lost that she couldn't ... you know, snippets here and there.

Malka explains, "It was just this unspoken-of thing that hung over my dad and his parents... it was just this like unspoken-of, constant grief that was there." The grief "hung over" them in silence, a tenacious, intensifying silence, like thunderclouds gathering before a storm. Filled with electricity, the pressure ultimately struggles for release. Malka further reveals, "I was sensitive enough to know she'll share with me what she wants when she wants to because otherwise it wouldn't be such a big deal." Without her grandmother or father speaking a word, Malka understands the request to leave the past untouched and unspoken. It must be "such a big deal," Malka winds up thinking to herself, and history is transmitted through the authority of silence. As Kaplan (1996) writes of the second generation survivor: "At first the child knows only that one or both parents are hiding some terrible secret. And the child wonders, 'What is the meaning of the absence, the silence? What is the truth that must never be spoken?'" (p. 219). Malka, the third generation recipient of this knowledge, is the first to explore her "double life" existence, recognizing how events that occur in the present are filled with reverberations of things that happened in the past (Kaplan, 1996, p. 231). Along these lines, Malka questions her family's ability to remain silent even in the face of the "frightening" physical similarity between Malka and her great grandmother. Similarly, she reveals her father's ongoing fear of loss:

> My dad has dreams about losing us, his children, all the time. Like, all the time. Even now, dreams about losing us. I don't know if that's a common paranoid parent thing, but my dad throughout my childhood would come running into my room in the middle of the night to make sure I was still there. Even now, as an adult, when I'll randomly sleep over at my parents' place, he'll come in the middle of the night and make sure I'm still there.

Closed off from his awareness of history within the present, the historical trauma perseveres with force. Malka understands of her father, "Like, he clearly has dealt with his own trauma growing up. You know, there are classic signs of children who are Holocaust survivors and the shit that they deal with, and like he just is completely emotionally distant, but completely emotional at the same time." Interestingly, Malka discusses the "classic signs of children who are Holocaust survivors," pegging her father as a survivor of the Holocaust, not a descendant of survivors. Even as a second generation survivor, her father is felt to be a child survivor of the Holocaust. This terminology depicting future generations as "survivors" or "not survivors" reappears in a later discussion of Malka's own sense of fear:

> M: I think I'm a lot more aware of anti-Semitism. My husband's not even a Holocaust survivor, but grew up with a strong Zionist family, but left Russia when the government got bad and just like… this fear that we

don't... people can turn against you... you can think you're nice and cozy in the place where you live and then you're not so nice and cozy anymore.
N: Do you see that affecting the way you live, like the day-to-day type of things?
M: In a way, it does. I'm hyper aware of it. I'm hyper aware of the bias in the media. I'm hyper aware of how much we're hated. I just am, and I find it so ridiculous when people don't see that. It's like, yeah, we're Jews. We're hated.

Malka finds herself to be "hyper aware of how much we're hated," making up for generations of family members who chose not to be aware. For Malka, therefore, the bias, the fear, and the hate seem omnipresent. Malka's allocation of second and third generation survivors as "children who are Holocaust survivors" therefore speaks to her sense of closeness to the event. After all, although it occurred in the past, its impact and presence is tangible in the present. Throughout her interview, Malka questions and explores her family's detachment from the trauma, wondering how and why they repressed their histories. At the same time, however, Malka describes her family's inherent distance from the Holocaust during and immediately following the event itself. Because they were not themselves prisoners in the camps, and did not die during the event, her family by definition did not suffer in "the same way" as others:

M: It's just weird... because it's not talked about. It was... you know, in a way, they weren't in the camps, so it was this kind of transient trauma because they didn't have to... they lost their families so they couldn't have suffered the same way that their family did so it was this like, even more passed on. It was just so weird. You know, because they survived it but they didn't really. They weren't there.
N: They themselves probably felt very disconnected.
M: Yeah, they lost their family but they never knew what their family went through, so it's not like they can even fathom, and yet they have no one. You know what

I mean? So that kind of disconnect is a kind of survivor guilt, too. Like, I lost my whole family and I managed to… my family talked about that a little bit… how like why wasn't… like, her brother was eight and he was too young to go to sleep-away camp, and so he missed the boat. You know, like, "Why did I make it?" Because they were safe. They were very blessed that they didn't have to go through any of that.

N: Do you feel you have that kind of guilt that carries on, in terms of what you choose to do in the name of your family?

M: Well, yeah, of course. Like, where are we going to live, and how come we're not living in Israel, and like, why aren't we living the Zionist dream that our grandparents fought so hard for? You know. Why aren't we there when we should be there? But oh yeah, there's a total guilt of: are we being good Jews? Are we being good enough Jews? Are we giving the right things? Are we making all the sacrifices that all of our grandparents went through? Like, both sides of our family our grandparents ate shit, you know. They just did. They had a shitty, shitty, shitty life. You know. Our parents had a crappy life, too. They did. My mom had a happy childhood, but, like, they had nothing. You know. They had nothing. And for a lot of my childhood I felt very guilty. You know, she was like suck it up and deal with it. Learn to deal with it…

N: Like forever paying back something that you don't owe.

M: Yeah… Like, look at how much they suffered so they could be there and we're not there. Of course, I think it's something we'll always struggle with. Like, how do we live there? I mean, it's hard to live there. But in many ways it's just as hard not living there.

Malka says, "…they lost their families so they couldn't have suffered the same way that their family did, so it was this like, even more passed on. It was just so weird. You know, because they survived it but they didn't really." In this way, Malka links her grandparents' escape to their experience that they did not "really" survive, and to the ensuing "survival guilt" that remains. As Malka explains, "transient" trauma seems to be "even more passed on" because of its vague, indescribable nature. "...so it's not like they can even fathom, and yet they have no one," she says, meaning they did not witness the horrors of the Holocaust, yet they have also seen the horrors of the Holocaust quite directly. A sense of connection and disconnection to the traumatic event therefore co-exist, regardless of a survivor's specific circumstances. While Dori Laub (1992) explains that "there is no such thing as a witness" of the Holocaust because anyone with a true understanding of the event was killed, every survivor, escapee, and descendant of the Holocaust is simultaneously a carrier of the trauma in his or her own way. Malka describes the impact of her history on her present-day decisions; from where she lives and being a "good enough Jew," to maintaining a sense of Zionism and compensating for all those who "ate shit." In the same way, Malka captures the importance of transmitting the knowledge and the "utter loss" to her future children:

> ...everybody was killed in the Holocaust. It still gets to me. Of course it does. And I wonder how my children will feel about that; I wonder how they're gonna know about it; I wonder how much connected they're going to be to that notion of utter loss. I can only fathom it to a certain extent because I know what my grandmother went through. They won't know my grandparents. They won't know what it's like to have lost... you know, that whole concept is going to be lost to them, and how do you pass that on? Not that you want to savor it, but there's something that's so important about our history as people, you know, and I think maybe that's why I have such... maybe that's why we've always been such Zionists, too. No matter what, what does my father-in-law say? Like, "Israel's like your child with special needs... you love it, it has problems, but you've got to keep it." Like, there's something... you need to have that country because things happen and people hate Jews. And that was something that was just known. It was something that was just passed on... it was like, people will hate you

and people will kill you and you can lose everything you have in a second—don't ever think it can't happen. And that was why you need this country to exist. You don't need to live there, but it has to exist. And it has to be there and it has to be safe, because at the end of the day that's really the only place you can go when the shit hits the fan.

"Not that you want to savor it, but there's something that's so important about our history as people," Malka perceptively states, comprehending the importance of memory and the intergenerational transmission of history. The fear that her children "won't know what it's like to have lost," however, is a needless one, as they will undoubtedly receive this knowledge from their mother on some level. "Savoring" the existence of memories and willingly exploring their knowledge is less of a certainty. Alongside her history "as people," Malka simultaneously hopes to transmit a sense of safety and belonging that she attained through Zionism and a love of Israel. As she quotes, "Israel's like your child with special needs… you love it, it has problems, but you've got to keep it." Thus, alongside her past, Malka passes on the potential for a rewarding present and future.

CHAPTER 11: JESSICA

Without Memory or Desire

The act of acknowledging, exploring, and expressing her own experiences allows a granddaughter of survivor(s) to more fully comprehend her history. That is, she must not have sorted through historical tales in order to construct a family narrative; the ability to recognize her past depends entirely upon her willingness to engage with her self in the present. What occurs when a young woman finds value in blocking her feelings and experiences? What of the individual and collective memories? Jessica, the 23-year-old granddaughter of a Holocaust survivor and the sister of another interviewee, explains:

> J: It's weird... I feel like I'm really bad at remembering my childhood. Like, some people remember all of the details. I'm really like, vague on it, but I feel like what sticks out is just her... like, she would yell a lot—like, *scary* yelling. Like, I feel like people are like, "Oh, yeah, my mom yells," like, whatever... but it's like the combination of the look in her eyes and the tone and like, how she would yell, was, like, scary. And I was like... I guess that when it started, like, I would block it out. Like, my sister, when my mom would yell at her she would cry... which is, like, normal, but I would just stare at her.
> N: You wouldn't cry?
> J: Yeah.
> N: So you kind of survived it by not focusing on it?
> J: Yeah, exactly. And I don't even know what she was screaming about. Like, when I think about it now, I'm like, what could I have done to evoke such anger?

Whether or not Jessica recognizes that she is not herself the root of such rage, she contemplates ways she might have "evoked such anger."

After all, a child will first and foremost blame herself for events she cannot understand. In explaining how anger impacts her today, Jessica reveals, "Like, when these other things happen, I get upset because it's me... like it's my fault... like I caused this to happen..." Her mother's "*scary* yelling," therefore, speaks to the severity of her mother's anger as well as Jessica's belief that she is single-handedly powerful and destructive enough to cause this eruption. In all its intensity, the experience is incomprehensible and staggering to Jessica within the present-day context; after all, the extent of her mother's fury relates to years of pent-up anger and frustration, having served as a caretaker for two traumatized, volatile, suicidal parents. Thus, its immensity could not be taken in, but rather needed to be blocked out. "I would just stare at her," Jessica says, creating in me the image of a hollow, plastic replica of Jessica sitting dispassionately before her shouting mother, untouched by her blows. The ability to dissociate was a powerful and valuable tool throughout Jessica's childhood, one that protected her from her mother's emotional flood, the ever-present traumatic past, and Jessica's own sense of helplessness and destructiveness. At the same time, it seems that alongside her dissociations, Jessica simultaneously lost track of her life experiences. This hazy and elusive sense of the world continues in her day-to-day life: "I feel like it's hard to hold onto things. Things that, like, my friends remember. Like, today they were giving the pre-nursing exam and I'm just like, 'What was on that?' It wasn't that long ago and I can barely remember?"

In sharp contrast to her self-depiction as a non-crying, detached little girl, Jessica opens her interview with the statement "Okay, I'm probably going to cry." Within moments she is in tears, sharing freshly acquired insights regarding her mother's denial of emotions (except for, as it turns out, anger), and her own attempts to foreclose feelings:

> J: I recently started going to therapy. I talk about my mom a lot. I feel like she doesn't show her emotions a lot and she equates that with being strong. And I talked to her also recently for one of my psych classes about... I just like interviewed her and we ended up talking about her dad and like the Holocaust and stuff like that and... I think she equates not showing emotions with being strong... like he had to be strong to get through that.

And that's what she thinks being strong is: like, not showing any emotions. I never realized before, but when I started therapy I realized that my whole life I've been like holding back my emotions, like, bottling everything up inside... so I think that in that way that's how it's affected me.

N: So how has it been in therapy?

J: It's really hard because now I feel like I'm overflowing with emotions... like, I need to find like a balance. Like, every time I go to therapy I cry the entire time. So, eventually, I am hoping I can find a happy medium. Like, not bottling everything up and not crying all of the time.

"...he had to be strong to get through that," Jessica states, revealing an entrance-point of the past in the present, manifesting itself in this family's sense of the word "strong": "I feel like she doesn't show her emotions a lot and she equates that with being strong." The emotionless mother is reminiscent of Jessica's dissociative childhood self, as this self-protective quality was transmitted through the generations. However, the meaning of the word "strong" is certainly altered depending on scale and context; maintaining strength during the Holocaust in a concentration camp is incomparable to exhibiting strength in a post-Holocaust world. With the help of therapy, Jessica successfully begins to break out of incongruous classifications and beliefs.

"It's really hard because now I feel like I'm overflowing with emotions," she says, regaining access to an abundance of feelings denied for generations by preceding, "strong" family members. Having been barred release for so long, the expression of feelings understandably erupts without "balance," pouring out in excess. Most certainly, these feelings belong to Jessica: after "bottling everything up" throughout her life, she courageously discovers how to express herself. At the same time, however, these feelings belong to her mother, her father, her grandparents, and every family member unable to communicate his or her emotions. For the first time, Jessica breaks down the emotional barriers that previously prevented her from seeking an authentic expression of her self.

Jessica describes the measures taken by her mother to not display the slightest trace of sadness: "...sometimes you can see her getting upset, but she'll never admit she's upset or just let it out. Like, she'll just be like, 'Oh, my allergies...' like if her eyes are getting watery." In describing her mother as "not showing emotions" or unable to "admit she's upset," Jessica sheds light on her mother's incessant anger, often an enactment of the avoided underlying feelings. In other words, her mother's lack of emotional expression helped generate her later explosions. Unsurprisingly, with anger running rampant throughout her life, Jessica continuously struggles to escape its force:

> J: Yeah, I feel like that's how I am now. Like, I put everything on me. Like, the way people act towards me affects me so much. Even though rationally I know like they're having a bad day and that's like their stuff... but it affects me so much, which is really hard right now because one of my instructors is kind of not so nice and it's really hard for me to not take it personally.
> N: So someone else gets angry and you feel like it's your doing?
> J: Yeah, and I can't handle people being angry. Like, I can handle it, but not well. Just even, like, strangers... a bus driver once yelled at me but like... he was letting people on without paying and I didn't realize it and paid, and he like kind of yelled at me. And something like that just like ruins my entire day. I feel like other people can just like brush it off.

Jessica cannot simply "brush it off" because anger is a heavily loaded emotion in her history. Therefore, seemingly minor expressions of anger, like a bus driver yelling at her for paying the fare, has the power to ruin Jessica's entire day. After all, any anger directed at Jessica serves as a reenactment of her early childhood experience; the bus driver becomes like her mother, and in seconds Jessica is transformed into a frightened, destructive, and guilty little girl. Jessica struggles to explain why she tends to "put everything" on herself, speaking not only about her relationship with her mother and others around her, but also about a sense of responsibility for her family's traumatic history. In later describing her "issues with people not liking" her, Jessica once again addresses her own mistreatment while alluding to her family's past persecution:

CHAPTER ELEVEN

> I feel like that's one thing I'm working on more in therapy because I feel like I never realized it before (crying)... but when I think about it, it's like obvious that I have issues with people not liking me... like, I want everyone to like me, so I won't say anything cause I don't want them to be mad at me. Well, I'm bad with people being mad at me. So I just feel like maybe they won't like me anymore. And, like, in therapy we brought that back to my mom getting angry, and another aspect of her getting angry is that when she gets mad about something she holds onto it forever and ever and ever. And it'll be like months and months later and she'll bring it up.

Jessica's description reveals that not only was she the recipient of anger in the heat of an angry moment, but her mother clung to every transgression "forever and ever and ever." Thus, Jessica was never free from the firm grasp of her mother's fury, awaiting a recurrence of the situation "months and months later," unable to find comfort at the conclusion of an eruption, always living in the presence of dis-ease. Understandably, Jessica's anxiety level was heightened. Yet, even in her constant state of anxiety, Jessica worked hard to suppress her discomfort:

> I feel like I've been dealing with anxiety by like not feeling it kind of. I just like push it down. Because now I realize I'm a very anxious person. Like, anxious about exams and about clinical... and, like, now that I think about it, I always had nerves about doing new things, even if they're not new, like going to camp every summer. Like, I love camp, but just like the change of it was like I always get an upset stomach. So nerves like, yeah, that's how my anxiety always comes up... with an upset stomach instead of like... it came out physically, my anxiety.

As she describes "not feeling" her anxiety and finding ways to "push it down" served to eliminate Jessica's conscious awareness of her anxiety for some time. Unconsciously, her anxiety was intense and unwavering, finding expression in various forms, sometimes physically, as Jessica says, and other times through her dreams:

N: Do you have nightmares?
J: Well, occasionally, but not, like, Holocaust related.
N: Any that stand out or any recurring ones?
J: One that stands out is I feel like I had a dream where there was this overarching like voice—kind of maybe like the voice of God, but not God, because it was evil and kind of like trying to kill me. And there was like a wall and it kept getting closer.
N: So then what happened?
J: I always wake up before I either escape or get squished.
N: So you've had that dream more than once.
J: Maybe more than once, or someone trying to kill me. Not often though...
N: Maybe with the wall closing in, feeling a little stuck...?
J: I have like, anxiety dreams all the time. Like where I'm supposed to be in a million places at once.
N: And you can't get there?
J: Like in once place and then I realize I'm supposed to be someplace else *and* someplace else. And the dreams where you're like late for school and stuff like that.

Jessica's "anxiety dreams" allow some of her tension to be released during sleep, whether she is "supposed to be in a million places at once," the "voice of God" is trying to kill her, or a wall keeps "getting closer" until she gets "squished." While releasing tension in her sleep in no way eliminates her waking anxiety, the dreams allow some of her "not felt" feelings to be expressed. Furthermore, her recollection of these dreams reveals her ability to hold onto some feelings and bring them into consciousness. Finally, her verbal recounting of her dream life plants the dreams in her waking narrative. Thus, the dreams provide an opportunity for Jessica to reflect on the arising feelings—if she chooses to do so—without having to recognize and acknowledge them in her daily life. However, Jessica's proclamation that her nightmares are not "Holocaust related" reiterates her tendency to not fully want to know. After all, moments earlier, Jessica described her mother and grandfather's Holocaust-related nightmares:

> J: My mom said he would scream in the middle of the night from nightmares about it.
> N: What about your mom? Did she have nightmares?
> J: Not that I know of. Like, I asked her during our conversation if she could tell me things that he would tell her, but she wouldn't tell me because she said, "You'll have nightmares."

Jessica finds herself "stuck" somewhere between past and present, between knowing and not knowing. While she may not *want* to know the full meaning of her mother's nightmares or her own, it seems that she *does* on some level know, evoking the notion of the "unthought known" (Bollas, 1989). "Well, occasionally, but not like Holocaust related" she tells me, reassuring herself that she has escaped the family pattern of Holocaust-related nightmares, and that her struggles are separate from this history. Yet, without hearing her grandfather's Holocaust stories or tracing his experiences on a historical timeline, Jessica's family narrative and collective identity inevitably revolve around this historical, traumatic event. At the core of her nightmares, her "bad" memory, and her search for answers, the Holocaust is ever-present.

Reconstructing Memory

The enormous amount of not-knowing Jessica utilized in order to survive her childhood was likely a useful tool within an unknowable, unreachable family. Jessica describes fragments of memories within a memory-less past:

> J: ...I think her and my dad went to therapy together when I was younger, when I was like nine. Like, I feel like I remember them leaving the house once a week at night and I feel like they weren't going out to dinner... and they were like yelling a lot during a certain period of time.
> N: So no one ever told you that? You pieced it together?
> J: Yeah, no one told me they were going to therapy.
> N: Do you feel like you had to do that a lot? Sort of like fragments... putting the fragments together, figuring things out?

J: I feel like that's the only thing I had to put together because everything else was so well hidden from me that I wouldn't know if like someone told me. But even when my mom told me she was always running off to like put my grandmother in the hospital or get her out of the hospital… even when she told me, it wasn't like, "Oh, that makes sense, you were running around." It wasn't like that. It was like, "Really?" I just had no idea. Like, I don't remember her running around. Like, she tells me that she would leave me with like her best friend, who I used to think I was related to, but like I don't remember. I feel like the first time I went to therapy I said that I'm really bad at remembering things and she implied that that's a defense mechanism to just not remember it.
N: And what do you think about that?
J: I think that that makes sense to me. Like, to me it doesn't feel like something I'm doing intentionally.

Instead of feeling abandoned, terrified, and in the dark about her parents' whereabouts, Jessica blocked out the experience of her missing parents altogether. By the time her mother explained that her absence was caused by "running off" to take care of her grandmother, Jessica had completely erased the experience, allowing her to state, "I don't remember her running around." Her mother's best friend, whom Jessica saw frequently enough to believe that this woman was a relative, has been completely blocked from Jessica's recollections. Time spent with this woman throughout Jessica's childhood has been altogether erased. Indeed, the defense mechanism of "not remembering" is not an "intentional" response to her upbringing; after all, intentionality suggests active, purposeful doing or thinking. Instead, Jessica's experience has been characterized by avoidance, denial, and dissociation from her surroundings, as she resiliently learned to enclose herself in the safety of not-knowing.

As discussed above, Jessica is by no means the first in her family to utilize the tool of not-knowing. For example, Jessica introduces the word "oblivious" in the following story:

> My mom said like that my grandma would stay in bed all

CHAPTER ELEVEN

day and not do anything. And my grandpa would come home from work and he would think that she just had gone to bed... like she had gotten up and done whatever. So she said he was oblivious to her in general, like, her sickness.

In remaining oblivious, unaware, and unconscious of his wife's illness, her grandfather was able to never truly know his wife's experience. What might he have found, had he chosen to see? What might Jessica discover in removing her shield of oblivion? Would she unearth the impact of having been abandoned by her mother on most days of her childhood? Might she expose the role of the Holocaust on her individual and family narrative? Could she tolerate the accompanying feelings?

While many generations of Jessica's family engaged in ongoing enactments and repetitions without further curiosity or exploration, Jessica courageously found her way into therapy. She explains her ability to do so with the following:

> J: Something happened and basically I felt like I was being overly emotional about it. Like, I didn't know why I was that upset about it... so that's when I started going to therapy. Basically it was just emotions from everything that had built up and was coming out now.
> N: It's really amazing you could get yourself into therapy.
> J: Like, I thought about it for a while but then kept not actually doing it because I thought I could survive without it. I think I will benefit from it. That's another reason why I didn't go to therapy: I didn't want to think that I needed help. Like, I could handle it myself, which is like, from my mom, I think.

Once again, the past is alive within the present, encouraging Jessica's mother, and later Jessica, to learn to "survive" without help. While they could clearly "survive without it," as her mother proved throughout her life, "survival" is most simply defined as a "continued existence" (and the antonym of "survival" is "death"). Thus, this terminology implies a basic, physical survival, one reminiscent of Jessica's grandfather's survival in the concentration camps. Furthermore, the words "overly emotional" reveal Jessica's belief that within a specific scenario, she responded with an excess of feeling beyond the scope of that situation. Jessica explains, "Basically it was just emotions from everything that had built up and was coming out now." Indeed, Jessica is "overly emotional," carrying three generations' worth of unexpressed feelings "that had built up" over time. When she concludes the interview by comparing the interview experience to therapy, Jessica reveals: "Like, every time I go to therapy... I'm just gonna cry. Like, I should be prepared to cry. Cause I used to go and like, 'I feel good, this week was good, like, I don't think I'm gonna cry.' But I would anyway." That is, Jessica's tears have nothing to do with the present—with whether or not "this week was good"—and everything to do with working through generations of past trauma.

In addition to the incessant flow of tears, talk therapy is an experience altogether deviating from Jessica's lifetime of silence:

> J: My dad is like super mellow. My mom's the one screaming her head off and my dad just sits there, like I would just sit there.
> N: So you're more like him?
> J: Yeah, I feel like we're both really quiet. My therapist suggested calling him more, but it's kind of weird because we're both quiet and we'll just sit there in silence.
> N: So what is your silence about?
> J: To me, it just feels like I don't have anything to say. Like, other people have asked me, "Why are you so quiet?" And I'm just like, "Why do you talk so much?"

Jessica describes how her father "just sits there," similarly attempting to block his wife's shrieks. Not surprisingly, in the face of a mother "screaming her head off" and a father retreating into silence, Jessica feels, "I don't have anything to say." Organizing or even recognizing her thoughts and feelings seems exhausting, if not impossible, within this chaos, and Jessica consequently assumes "silent" and "shy" as safe descriptions of her personality. In exploring the role of silence, her family's foreclosure of feelings, and her own trouble with memory, Jessica uncovers her individual identity as well as a historically-insightful family narrative.

In addition to therapy, Jessica has discovered alternative ways to examine, question, and make sense of her childhood. Most significant is her experience of babysitting:

> N: And doing things differently as a mom… do you ever think about how you would want to be as a mom, or is there anything you would do differently from your mom with your kids?
> J: Yeah, I thought about that a little and especially I feel like in therapy… I've talked about how the moms I baby-sit for are with their kids also. Like, one of them sometimes reminds me of my mom and the other one never… I think is the best mom ever and I would never… like, I've been babysitting for them for a while and I've spent a lot of time when the mom is there—like if they don't go out right away—and I just realized that I admire how she is with her child. Like, she's just so patient and just, like, so calm and I hope I can be like that.
> N: It must be so strange to see a mom like that.
> J: It's like, wow.

Through babysitting, Jessica hopes to better understand what it means to be a mother in general, and her own mother specifically. She encounters fragments of her mother in other mothers, and is able to analyze them from a safe distance. Furthermore, in witnessing other mother-daughter dynamics, Jessica hopes to more fully know herself. For example, she reveals, "I talked about it in therapy—like the mom of the two girls, she'll yell about something if the little one spills food at the table… like the tone of her voice is familiar. And in my head I'm like, all she did was an accident and she's like five." Thus, within the context of "babysitting," Jessica is able to examine her upbringing, her mother's misplaced rage, and the prospect of herself as an innocent child undeserving of blame or reprimand. Like therapy, babysitting provides Jessica with an opportunity to engage in new relational possibilities in an unencumbered space. Of course, Jessica will continue to contend with her earliest relationships throughout her life; yet, having mentioned "therapy" over a dozen times in her interview and sought out therapeutic activities, it seems Jessica has begun the meaningful work of self-exploration.

CHAPTER 12: BRIANA

It's Not You, It's Me

Briana, a 22-year-old granddaughter of Holocaust survivors, articulately captures the evolution of emotional blunting within her family:

> My grandparents on my dad's side were both Holocaust survivors and the first result I think I saw, or was conscious of, was probably depression throughout the family in the second generation, and people not wanting to share their feelings or expressing feelings or expressing love verbally, and hearing stories about how my grandparents never said, like, "Good job," or "You're good enough." It was more like, "You're not good enough," because they didn't feel good enough because they felt like they shouldn't have survived. They felt a lot of guilt for surviving. So it trickles down to the third generation, I think, through the parents, the second generation—having to deal with how they grew up and not knowing how to change it.

Through the use of projection and introjection, Briana's father and grandparents demonstrate the conscious and unconscious transmission of trauma intergenerationally. As Briana insightfully explains, her grandparents communicated the message "'You're not good enough,' because they didn't feel good enough because they felt like they shouldn't have survived." In this way, survival guilt was passed on to Briana's father—also not "good enough"—resulting in "depression throughout the family" and "people not wanting to share their feelings or expressing feelings or expressing love verbally." Later on, Briana adds, "I think anger is also heavily present, not just like depression... like, anger with my dad, anger with my aunt, and my uncle also..." That is, various family members utilized anger, often an enactment of undigested, avoided emotion. As Briana describes growing up with a father who struggled to verbalize his love for her, she recalls her attempts to understand his lacking emotional displays, as well as to repair the injury of his own withholding parents.

> I think we saw my dad as being emotionally aloof, like we noticed he wouldn't say the same things my mom was capable of saying, like verbalizing or showing... we were always told by our mom that it's not about us, it's about how he grew up and his parents... and we would talk to my grandparents about it as little kids, like, "Why don't you tell Abba[1] you love him more?" And whatever, stuff like that.

The image of "little" Briana innocently attempting to mend the divide between her father and his parents is a compelling one. "Why don't you tell Abba you love him more?" she questions, capturing the essence of the void. Yet, how can expressions of "love" possibly survive the chaotic upheaval of emotions following massive psychic trauma? As Briana's mother emphasizes in an attempt to explain her husband's "aloof" nature, "it's not about us, it's about how he grew up and his parents..." In other words, history steers the present, such that "love" in the present remains intimately coupled with "love" for all who were lost. As Briana describes her father's household growing up: "... they say it was like dark and it was sad and like all they heard about was all the family members they didn't have anymore... like, who was missing, who wasn't there, and what a struggle it was... how lucky they were to be alive." Thus, "not knowing how to change it," Briana's father continues to exist within a "dark" and "sad" world, forever joined with those who are missing. In this consuming relationship with absence, he becomes himself an "absent" and "aloof" father, therefore deeming Briana a part of this cycle as well.

In an attempt to better understand this powerful *thing* which dominates her father's life and represents competition for fatherly attention, Briana recalls turning to her grandparents: "We asked them questions all the time when they came over. We asked them detailed questions. I think the second generation didn't do that apparently. Like, my dad wouldn't ask them questions, but like, all the grandchildren felt com-

---

[1] This is the Hebrew word for "father."

fortable." In struggling to comprehend her father and her family history through "detailed questions," Briana distinguishes herself from the second generation by feeling "comfortable"; that is, she eliminates the silence and attempts to understand, and maybe, one day, undo this *thing*. Furthermore, Briana recalls, "I remember talking to my grandparents about it a few times just because I was so upset about it, but I think we've ultimately accepted that, like, they did the best he could, he did the best they could." In Briana's confusion of pronouns, "… they did the best he could, he did the best they could," she seemingly concedes to the merger between her father, her grandparents, and their shared history. Later in her interview, Briana recounts the ways in which she "was so upset about it":

> I think it took a while to realize where I was coming from, like really realize, but it had to do with having a father who was absent and making it seem like you're not good enough all the time. I guess my siblings didn't internalize it as much as I did… just because I was very emotional and whatever, but I think as time went on it had to do more with my dad and not so much with the rest of my family. Like, it's difficult because I know it came from my grandparents who didn't really have a choice in how they dealt with their problems, and he didn't have a choice in how he had his childhood, but it definitely trickles down to the third generation.

Briana's self-image as "very emotional"—in contrast to her siblings, whom she believes "didn't internalize" their "absent" father as much as she did—is common amongst third generation survivors. In a sense, the collective, third generation identity revolves around an "overly emotional" self, whether owned or disowned. After all, as Briana reminds herself, her grandparents "didn't really have a choice in how they dealt with their problems" and her father "didn't have a choice in how he had his childhood." Therefore, because others suffered more deeply, harboring her own sense of loss or grief is regarded as exaggerated, often considered "too much" or labeled "overly" sensitive. Alongside her predecessors, however, Briana likewise "didn't really have a choice"; in later describing the various ways her siblings have dealt with their shared history, it seems Briana served as the "emotional" one for her ancestors, her siblings, and future generations alike:

> B: I think being an artist makes me overly expressive sometimes, but I definitely am not afraid to express what I'm feeling with my family or friends.
>
> N: Yeah, you've said that you are "overly expressive" and "overly emotional." Is that what people call you or do you just feel very expressive?
>
> B: I think my older sister was very protective when we were little… with bad relationships going on with my brother and my dad… and so she kind of put up this stronghold on the family and didn't show how it was affecting her. But I on the other hand was really little and so I cried about it all the time and was very expressive, particularly of what I was expressing. But then as time went by, I went to therapy and realized what the problems were… like, eventually, after a long time, I decided I needed to open up to the family and think about, like, why I had issues and maybe was dealing with them but not in a very direct way. And so I talked to my brother and my sister and my mom about what went on in my family for me in terms of my dad. I never really talked to my dad about it.
>
> N: I'm amazed. How did that go?
>
> B: Well, my mom always wanted to be let in throughout the therapy process, but I, like, refused to and it took me a long time to be able to open up to her about it, which was difficult for her. And then my older sister was away from home the whole time and she wanted to know more about it but I didn't open up that much to her about it… and then, in like the middle of college, my brother finally said that he wanted to know about what had gone on because he also had not been home, so I finally opened up to him about all of it. I think it was a shock for him to realize about how much my dad had affected me or how much the family had affected me, but I also thought he needed to know about it because God forbid one of his

kids had some sort of problem and he had some knowledge because he had a sister with the same problem.
N: They couldn't see how it was affecting you or how it might be affecting them…
B: I think to some degree it was foreign to them. I think they have their guard up and I don't. They're able to be much more closed and I'm not.
N: What do you think it is about you?
B: I think it's the artist thing. I'm really emotional, like I don't really know how to keep a guard up—it just kind of all comes in. I don't know how to filter out the emotions. I'm very sensitive. I think my siblings are sensitive too, but they are really able to like not talk about their feelings and be okay, and I'm just kind of not like that.

As the "overly expressive" member of her family, Briana depicts letting each family member in on "what went on" for her growing up in their family. Playing the role of the "sensitive," "artist" sister who does not "really know how to keep a guard up" or "how to filter out emotions," it is clear that Briana serves as the unguarded, open, and honest communicator of their shared experiences. While Briana believes of her brother "it was a shock for him to realize about how much my dad had affected me or how much the family had affected me," she alludes to knowledge that there may have been more at play for her siblings than they let on: of her sister, she recalls "… she kind of put up this stronghold on the family and didn't show how it was affecting her…" That is, a "stronghold" allowed her sister to maintain a sense of order and control. Along these lines, Briana later reveals her sister's own attempts to engage with her history:

B: We've all been back to Poland… like my three siblings… not my parents. But we definitely saw the concentration camps. My sister even went back to my grandma's house that she grew up in. We've definitely all been back there to see it.
N: How was that?
B: Very hard. I actually didn't cry the whole trip… the only time in my life I haven't cried… just because I think

it's too much. My sister is actually going into Holocaust studies... she's getting a masters in Israel. She's working at a Holocaust museum.
N: So it sounds like she and your brother are figuring things out without the emotional piece...
B: Yeah. She gets connected to it differently... I don't even think she's recognized it's affected her personality or her relationships with other people. Any issues she's had with boys, I don't think she's connected that with how my dad treated her.

As Briana insightfully explains, her sister "gets connected to it differently," enveloping herself in Holocaust studies and working with Holocaust material, as if separate from her personality. Thus, while her siblings seemed to "not talk about their feelings and be okay," they found alternate, intellectualized outlets for their experience. Briana therefore serves as the elected emotional expresser, the bearer of feelings and disarray, for her family. Furthermore, although Briana maintains conflicting feelings about having "cried about it all the time," she also captures the strength of her ability in her statement, "I definitely am not afraid to express what I'm feeling with my family or friends." In other words, her courage allows her to do the emotional work that others feared before her, and continue to fear alongside her. Perhaps her brother's "shock," therefore, also relates to his amazement with Briana's candidness and strength; the same amazement I felt as I listened to the role she plays and the work she has done in her family.

Briana understands that the transmission of history will not end with her generation. Regarding sharing her experiences with her brother, she states, "I also thought he needed to know about it because God forbid one of his kids had some sort of problem and he had some knowledge because he had a sister with the same problem." That is, Briana predicts that the current patterns and "problems" will persevere. At the same time, however, it seems that Briana has successfully opened the door to honest dialogue between her siblings. She reveals, "Yeah, we all talk about it a lot. We make promises not to do certain things he does... we analyze his siblings... we want to just get along and stuff like that." Hoping to do "certain things" differently from her father, and from his family altogether, Briana and her siblings promise one another to "just get along." This hope for the future is further actualized within a foundation of open conversation and awareness. As Briana emphasizes, "But I definitely want to think about a lot of the things like my dad did when I was growing up, and like change how I interact with my kids, and be very different than that."

It's Not Me, It's You

To what extent will Briana "be very different" as a parent than her father, if the patterns have been initiated and the dynamics persevere? How many more generations will receive the message "it's not about us, it's about how he grew up"? Or worse, how many will not make the historical connection in the first place? In a sense, the vague but ever-present place of history can be better understood through Briana's depiction of her father's roundabout insults: "It's probably from their parents always saying bad things instead of positive, but like they're very conscious of, 'It wasn't an insult, I'm just saying...' or like, 'Don't take it personally, but...'" The experience of passive yet aggressive, "mean" insults is like the back-handed subsistence of history within the present: indirect but personal, subtle but strong, seemingly shallow but deeply impacting.

Briana reveals how contending with her history remains an ongoing, inescapable challenge, for example through her grappling with anorexia: "So, I struggled with it for three years of high school. And my parents were really supportive in getting help and my dad... it was really hard for him to see. I think he knew he had something to do with it. I think my mom also felt guilt about it which didn't help with the guilty situation..." Briana openly links her eating disorder to her father, his upbringing, and the historically-relevant, ongoing "guilty situation." Briana goes on to share her parents' attempts not to "see" her disease:

> B: I definitely had to tell them. I think it's also... now it's more common knowledge—if you see someone who's underweight, you kind of freak out about it. But then, my mom... just thought I wanted to be better looking or whatever it was. But after like a good seven months, I was so frustrated that she didn't see it that I shouted at her that I needed help and convinced her that I needed

CHAPTER TWELVE

help... and my friends had to convince her I needed help...
N: So she really didn't want to see it.
B: Yeah. Then we had to approach my dad. He wanted to talk about it... not really talk about it... but he wanted to make me eat. Like, "You're not allowed to talk about it with me, you're not allowed to discuss it," and it put a halt on our relationship for a while. He didn't want to discuss the problem underlying it; he just wanted to fix it on the surface.
N: Make you eat.
B: Yeah.
N: So how bad did it get?
B: It wasn't like dire but... by the time the pediatrician found out, she was like, "She needs to eat immediately and take care of this." I think they were scared, well, I don't think my parents ever understood what... but it was a scary situation because it was so new to everyone. But I opened up about it pretty fast because I think I wanted to get better because I didn't want to continue this forever and the therapist was really good...

"I was so frustrated that she didn't see it that I shouted at her that I needed help and convinced her that I needed help... and my friends had to convince her I needed help..." Briana recalls, shedding light on the extent to which her family was unable and unwilling to see Briana and her experience. Furthermore, her father's inability to tolerate an honest verbal exchange is apparent in his complete rejection of his daughter and their relationship: "...but he wanted to make me eat. Like, 'You're not allowed to talk about it with me, you're not allowed to discuss it,' and it put a halt on our relationship for a while." Her father's immense sense of guilt and fear is tangible, as he was unable to tolerate the situation but rather wanted to be rid of it: through his demand "you're not *allowed*," her father clearly begs, "don't say it *aloud*." Briana's own sense of guilt for creating another "scary situation" emerges in her comment, "I didn't want to continue this forever." Her word choice—to "want to continue this forever"—suggests a deliberate maintenance, as though she developed the eating disorder on purpose. Perhaps this intentionality speaks to Briana's sense of competition with history, which regularly absorbs her father's attention, and which will undoubtedly last "forever."

Another example of history continuously presenting itself in Briana's life can be seen in her frightening dreams about the Holocaust:

> B: For as long as I can remember, I always had dreams about the Holocaust—usually like hiding and being terrified of being found, not really like fighting back or anything... I think my siblings have also struggled with dreams of the Holocaust.
> N: So you were hiding?
> B: Yeah. With like people we know.
> N: And you've had them since you were a little girl?
> B: Yeah, I remember being like eight or nine. I was with another friend and we talked about how we all had dreams like that and we were so terrified. It was such a central part of my childhood. I was so scared of it.
> N: So how is it now?
> B: It's still scary but it's so commonplace now it's not like a jolt anymore.
> N: Would it be on random nights or do you think something specific happened...?
> B: Sometimes random nights... sometimes something will be bothering me and it will come out in terms of the Holocaust. I remember last year, I was feeling really guilty about something or I thought I should feel guilty about it, and it came out in the way of the Holocaust and Nazis being around and being buried alive... it's like the imagery I use of the scariest thing I can think of.

Briana's awareness that things "come out in terms of the Holocaust" allows her to more fully explore and understand her experiences. While she describes how "the Holocaust and Nazis being around and being buried alive" serve as "imagery" to convey her feelings, she also captures the way in which these images impact and intensify her emotions. Her comments "It was such a central part of my childhood" and "I was so scared of it" depict the extent to which the past can come alive within the present. Feeling "terrified" and "jolt"-ed, she ultimately discusses

CHAPTER TWELVE

her dreams with siblings and friends, such that the historical trauma grows yet another root in her conscious day-to-day life. Along similar lines, Briana traces the meaning of "goodbye" within the "Holocaust mentality" of her post-Holocaust world:

> ...like when we say goodbye to people or when things end, we're extremely upset about it. It's like the whole Holocaust mentality. Whenever we said goodbye to our grandparents, they got very emotional because they thought of goodbye as, "That could be the end." So it was embedded in us that goodbye was the biggest deal in the world; if one of our friends go away we get very tense.

Briana's ability to link her eating disorder, nightmares, and "goodbyes" to her history allows her to maintain a more comprehensive understanding of her past, and to live more fully in the present. In her romantic relationships, for example, Briana describes discovering her desire for "emotionally available and open-hearted" men:

> I think I try to go the opposite of my dad, and there are times where I consciously went for the exact same kind of person as my dad, realized it pretty fast... he showed a lot of the same characteristics and I kind of ran away to some degree. But I definitely analyze like every guy that comes into the picture... with my mom, also. Like, "Do you see any characteristics that are the same? If so, what are they?" Like if they're similar, I shouldn't be with him...

Ultimately, Briana's self-exploration and historical curiosity facilitate her differentiation between the characteristics and desires that belong to her, and those that belong to her ancestors. Instead of continuously hearing "It's not you, it's me" and struggling to understand the meaning of this distinction, Briana is able to take on the assertion herself: "It's not me, it's you." After all, she alone can confirm or dispute the deepest parts of herself. In her final depiction of what is most distinctly hers—her name—Briana describes the "strong willed" woman she is named for:

B: We talk a lot about who we're named after, what their characteristics were, why we were named after them… we realized that's how we want the same thing for our kids…
N: Who are you named after?
B: I'm named for my mom's side—her grandmother.
N: And what were her characteristics?
B: She was like an immigrant from Russia; she was apparently very strong-willed. And her husband had come here first but then never sent for her. And she already had like four kids, so she just got on the boat by herself and came over here—no money and nowhere to go—but she somehow found him, had three more kids with him, and then they got divorced and she had all the seven kids alone. She raised them all herself; never got remarried. But she was very charitable, giving, also kind of a harsh mother, I think, but definitely strong willed.

As she continues to "raise" her family by doing their emotional work as well as her own, Briana quite powerfully exhibits the strength of will, vigor, and generosity of her namesake.

CHAPTER 13: DISCUSSION

Reworking Trauma Trails: Possibilities for Resilience

> Working on meaning is the most private of activities. Anything that has been imprinted with a trauma will always fuel representations of the memories that constitute our inner identity. That meaning lives on inside us and provides our life with its themes (Cyrulnik, 2007, p. 18).

Through psychoanalytic interviews with the granddaughters of Holocaust survivors, I uncovered in this work the themes which organize the lives of ten women. While the particulars of each woman's narrative and viewpoint are unique given the circumstances of her individual and family history, one constant truth persists throughout the narratives: that trauma trails exist within third generation survivors—whether conscious or unconscious—and are embodied in their day-to-day lives. Thus, the imprints of trauma which "constitute our inner identity" prevail; with or without conscious awareness, with or without our predecessors' attempts at reintegration into the world, with or without our rummaging into history in search of answers. Yet, this is not to say that granddaughters of the Holocaust are necessarily debilitated by their links to history. Instead, trauma trails must be welcomed, explored, even fostered, for growth to be achieved. The case of Leah, for example, reveals how a strong, open, and hopeful young woman can maintain a protective screen that limits her from fully engaging with and reworking her traumatic history. Consequently, Leah relies upon obsessive-compulsive tendencies to provide her with a sense of order and control. Samantha, on the other hand, delves into her historically-rooted fears, hopes, and desires, arriving at an intergenerational viewpoint that anchors her identity within history and unfastens the grip of a previously unexamined past. As a result, Samantha nurtures growth, attains emotional insight, and initiates new life possibilities. As long as the offspring of survivors attempt to cut off their connection to intergenerationally transmitted trauma, they will undoubtedly *be owned by* residues of the past. Conversely, the study of meaning, the acknowledgment, exploration, and working through of trauma, will allow the granddaughters and future descendants of the Holocaust to *own* their histories and further integrate their identities.

Each of the ten interviewees exposed both the ongoing shadow of the Holocaust, and the strength and resilience she developed alongside her inherited traumatic history. After all, the act of narrating an evolving narrative is in and of itself a demonstration of progress: the intimate disclosures of individual feelings, memories, and beliefs cultivate the narrator's sense of self and simultaneously integrate the past, present, and future. Such developments signify the potential for growth and change, and speak to the hope inherent in each one's search for insight. As Cyrulnik (2007) explains,

> Narration becomes a way of working on meaning ... Sometimes the witness exists only in the imagination of the injured subject, who is talking to a virtual listener as he tells himself his story ... Memories of images pass through their minds, and they are framed by words that comment on them, explain them, hesitate and then begin to describe the scene by using other expressions. Thanks to this work, the narrative can slowly extract the event from the self (p. 37-38).

As the narrator begins "working on meaning," resilience is born. It is through verbalizing, sharing, and grappling with her own representations that the narrator discovers such activities to be increasingly bearable, and increasingly necessary. In this way, these ten interviewees courageously engaged with new narrative possibilities in an unencumbered space—some for the first time, others for the 100th time—revealing their wounds to themselves and reworking their identities.

Unfortunately, a common misperception regarding change in a post-Holocaust world suggests that resilience is measured by the extent to which survivors and their families are able to reintegrate into society following this massive traumatic event. I often encounter women interested in my work who ask about my "findings," only to then half-frantically suggest why their particular family situation is different from the participants of my interviews. One woman assured me that *her* survivor grandparents did not seem troubled by their past; another revealed that *her* parents successfully made a place for themselves in society; a third explained why *her* family did not truly suffer through the Holocaust the way her neighbor's family did; and yet another woman maintained that *her* family was not impacted by the event generations later. Indeed, the thought that one cannot escape such an overwhelmingly traumatic history can be frightening, infuriating, and numbing all at once. To some extent, however, each of these women is right: some of their families appear to have made a 180-degree turn and begun a seemingly transformed, "successful" life. However, it is important to note that social achievements and change of circumstances do not necessarily indicate a reworking of trauma or a healing of internal suffering:

> When we draw up a balance for the last fifty years, we find that most Holocaust survivors did, despite everything, have families and become part of society once more ... Having had to fight so as not to go under helped them to succeed in life because they could dissociate their success from what was still a painful inner world ... All these examples of morbid courage explain why social success can go hand in hand with personal difficulties (Cyrulnik, 2007, p. 172).

As Cyrulnik explains, the distinction between one's "adaptation" to a post-Holocaust world and one's development of emotional "resilience" must not be overlooked:

> This form of adaptation may lead to success at school or in society, but it cannot be called resilience. Before we can speak of "resilience", the subject must begin to rework his idea of his wound in emotional terms. Now, the paradoxical success stories that exploit a psychotrauma by adapting to it do not rework any representations. This is not resilience and, what is more, this type of defence allows the psychotrauma to re-emerge at a later date; the subject thought it had been forgotten, but it had simply been avoided or buried (2007, p. 172-173).

Discussion

Misinterpretations and misrepresentations of healing are widespread. Avi Sagi-Schwartz, a prominent Holocaust researcher who has conducted quantitative studies and meta-analyses on the subject of intergenerational ties, repeatedly concludes from his researches that Holocaust trauma has not been transmitted to second or third generation offspring of survivors. One such study, for example, reports that:

> Holocaust survivors (now grandmothers) showed more signs of traumatic stress and more often lack of resolution of trauma than comparison subjects, but they were not impaired in general adaptation. Also, the traumatic effects did not appear to transmit across generations. Holocaust survivors may have been able to protect their daughters from their war experiences… (Sagi-Schwartz et al., 2003, p. 1086).

The notion that Holocaust survivors "successfully protected" their children from the influence of their traumatic past is contradicted by the findings of this work. The repetitive and evocative depictions of trauma trails amongst the third generation are very evident in the narratives of the current participants. On a more basic level, it seems unhelpful and dismissive to categorize a survivor who displays signs of traumatic stress as "not impaired in general adaptation." Sagi-Schwartz's understanding of "general adaptation" is limiting, and does not include the kind of complex understanding of "resilience" and "health" in a post-Holocaust world that my participants' interviews suggest.

Cyrulnik's (2007) perspective, on the other hand, is resonant with my own. Responding to Sagi-Schwartz's assertion that "the difficulties were definitely not passed on to their children," Cyrulnik is very clear on the limitations of a detached or apparently objective perspective:

> What does this mean? It means that personal interviews are more coherent than the findings of scientific research. Everyone was surprised to find that these young survivors were so successful. But if we talk to them about their subjective lives, we quickly discover that their emotional lives are disordered and that the schematic clarity

of social adventurism was the only thing that put them at their ease. In their heart of hearts, they experienced great sorrow. In order to stop themselves thinking that no one could love the living corpses they had become, that they exuded unhappiness and that they would communicate their unhappiness to those who deigned to love them, they took refuge in the only activity that prevented them from suffering. When they could do that, the rules of life were clear, and all they had to do was get up early, go to bed late and think of nothing but work. All they needed to follow the narrow path that led to social success was their courage. They ceased to suffer, and even found a certain peace, but the pain was never far away. They were saddened by their own emotional incompetence... (2007, p. 238).

Indeed, the emotional work of resilience is an immensely difficult venture. The challenge for members of the third generation of the Holocaust is heightened by the denial and dissociation of two preceding generations. Thus, the groundbreaking journey into one's history, filled with untouched, unexplored, seemingly "dangerous" emotions, can be a lonely and isolating endeavor. It is no surprise, therefore, that "3G" (third generation) groups have been launched, and within just a few years, have multiplied in popularity. This development reflects the continued coalescing of the third generation as an identifiable group, and the desire to unite in dialogue and reflection of what it means to identify as a third generation survivor. As the 3G NY website declares: "The mission of 3GNY is to serve as a living link between the history of the Holocaust and today" ("3GNY," n.d.). This "living link" is rooted in the community's pursuit of communication, education, and reflection. A "message from the group's steering committee" elaborates:

> We, the grandchildren of Holocaust survivors, come from diverse backgrounds and work in various fields, but we all share a unique family history. We are also the last living link to Holocaust survivors. It is only through us that future generations will know the actual stories of

> our grandparents' survival and the unimaginable losses of that generation.
> What will we tell them? How do we ensure that our grandparents' stories of loss, survival and hope are remembered? What is our legacy and how do we articulate it?
> By forming 3GNY, we sought to create a forum—a community—for grandchildren of Holocaust survivors where together we could answer these questions ...
> Ultimately, our coming together is about more than socializing. It is to decide the best ways of shaping and passing on the legacies of our grandparents and parents. As grandchildren of Holocaust survivors, it is vital we use our personal connection to bring to consciousness the realities and lessons of the Holocaust ("3GNY," n.d.).

Certainly, the lives of third generation survivors continue to be "steered" by their grandparents' past experiences. The ongoing questions—"What will we tell them? How do we ensure that our grandparents' stories of loss, survival and hope are remembered? What is our legacy and how do we articulate it?"—will undoubtedly persevere, both as individual and communal struggles. As long as the "realities and lessons" of the Holocaust are continuously brought to "consciousness," the case for resilience is hopeful. After all, it is only through such attempts that the most frightening parts of oneself and one's history are acknowledged and worked through. Likewise, while conducting these interviews, the compelling need for these women to impart their stories was palpable; by wrestling with history, they advanced on the route to self-knowledge and acceptance. As Kaplan reminds us, "The failure to mourn, to weep for the dead and for the unborn, guarantees a return of the repressed, until—one day—there is nothing but absence and silence, and no one to testify" (Kaplan, 1996, p. 237). This inquiry attempted to delve into the work of mourning, to battle absences with presences, and to resist the verdict of silence by creating a space for language. If it succeeded, the voices of these women will serve as an ongoing invitation to engage in open dialogue and self-reflection.

* * *

CHAPTER THRITEEN

On the day I designated for printing the initial draft of my dissertation, which would later form the basis of this book, I found myself catching a northbound train to complete the final preparations at my parents' home. Both my mother and father would be available, I knew, eager to lend a helping hand, possibly lessening my sense of isolation that had developed over the previous days. Upon my arrival, they heartwarmingly displayed their approval: of the conclusion of my research, of the significance of the subject matter, and of the tangible presence it aroused of my late grandmother. It had been approximately two months since her passing, with her death preceding the completion of my work by a mere eight weeks. The weight of her physical absence was colossal. I slumped down in the backward-facing bench of the train, knowing I was moving forward to my destination, yet willing the world to travel backwards in time to allow me to face my grandmother once more—with a copy of the manuscript in hand.

"Do you think she would have read this?" I asked my father, as we nervously watched the printer churn out page after page of my work in his upstairs office. "Oh, absolutely," he answered emphatically, and I felt momentarily at ease. I am not sure what sort of conclusion I had imagined for my research—perhaps a sense of organization or finalization or even validation—someone or something that could clarify the burdensome and conflicting feelings I bore throughout the process. In retrospect, I am aware of the ways in which this experience served as an essential step along my path of self-discovery, a path which transported me closer to my grandmother than ever before. My desire to pass the manuscript back to her, through the generations, stemmed from the hope that such a retroactive gesture might heal the wounds of trauma and silence. Nevertheless, the transformations of our shared history have undoubtedly begun. As I continuously cope with the knowledge I gather as well as the questions and absences that remain, I hope to interweave my trauma trails with an ongoing journey toward self-awareness and resilience.

EPILOGUE

Life Before This Study

> In order to become whole we must try, in a long process, to discover our own personal truth, a truth that may cause pain before giving us a new sphere of freedom. If we choose instead to content ourselves with "wisdom," we will remain in the sphere of illusion and self-deception (Alice Miller, 1997, p. 1).

As far back as I can remember, a yellow Star of David outlined in black with the words "Jude" sewn across its center hung in my grandparents' Jerusalem apartment. It was a small, cloth piece—small enough to walk past without noticing, particularly amidst the floor to ceiling bookshelves and distinct collection of artwork that lined the apartment.

Then again, it had always been framed.

As a young girl, I understood the glass covering as a statement about the unfairness of childhood and the plethora of adult decisions that I did not understand. There it hung, protected, calling out to me: "This bright, pretty star is not to be touched." It might have served as a soft doll blanket, I had thought—or a bold, taped-on addition to a crayon drawing of the evening sky. My parents would applaud my creativity, I imagined. Yet, the message was clear, and the last thing I wanted was to become a daring, questioning, potentially displeasing granddaughter. Someone else could bring it up.

Years passed, and the conversation never came. We continued our lives around that piece of memorabilia—eating meals at the table across from it, playing pick-up-sticks on the carpet beside it, admiring 1970's photographs my grandfather captured of Israeli soldiers praying at the Western Wall that hung alongside it. And, as I grew older, I no longer inspected the Star; I walked past it without awareness or desire, never questioning what it meant to live amidst this item, a symbol originally intended as a badge of shame associated with being a Jew.

Oh, I'm sure the Star was acknowledged on certain occasions—maybe on Holocaust Remembrance Day, or perhaps during Shabbat meals for which my grandparents' old friends had been invited to join. But the details surrounding the Star remained a mystery. Whose Star was it? Did one person wear it, or were Stars interchangeable amongst family members? What were the circumstances surrounding the receiving, wearing, and saving of that Star, and what was the journey that led it to its current home?

I did not ask these questions aloud and I never reflected on them in silence. It was as if the Star was not even there.

One Wednesday afternoon during my graduate school years, I sat in the office of my mentor, Dr. Michael O'Loughlin, discussing potential dissertation topics while seizing the opportunity to share childhood experiences and speak without boundaries. I did not think of the Star at the time, nor did I have words to explain my disjointed narrative. Yet I began to speak, and what surfaced was a reflection on familial silence, a subtle but powerful recognition of all that was and all that remained unsaid. And, somehow, without knowing it at the time, I spoke out of a deeply rooted longing—a hunger for truth and a hunger for pain—phenomena that were clearly intertwined in my mind, encouraging me for years to walk on by, to avoid a closer look, and to remain silent.

As I embarked on the "research" which ultimately led me to a doctoral dissertation and the present book, trauma and my vague understanding of "bearing witness" hovered nearby from the start; these were ambiguous concepts at first, ones that became increasingly defined through the process of a literature review, but which remained in the realm of "intellectual wisdom" until I began my interviews. While reviewing the Holocaust literature, I immersed myself in the material but also made certain to remain immensely busy with other tasks. I recall preparing to view a segment of the film *Shoah*, setting aside a couple of hours on a Sunday afternoon, knowing that I would subsequently clean my apartment and grocery shop prior to meeting my friends for dinner. I was aware of my need for structure in these moments: throwing myself into the material and the process, then throwing myself right back out of it. This was my approach at the time, seemingly satisfying my need to consume myself with the subject matter but also maintain my "separate" life.

Nevertheless, I felt nervous prior to beginning the interviews, as if I was asking participants to unload an entire history of a people and sit with the resulting discomfort. I fantasized about the potential outrage and disapproval that would surge out of participants who felt pressured or pushed or provoked by my questions, and viewed myself as an intrusive, unfeeling, demanding interviewer. I was instantaneously a young girl once more, fearing my family's response to my asking unspeakable questions and broaching forbidden themes. In these worried moments, it did not matter that my participants were willing individuals who had heard of my study and were interested in conversing on the subject matter.

As a way of sidestepping my anxieties, I busied myself with the concrete details surrounding the preparation of interviews. Would I welcome participants into my apartment, enter their home or office, or meet them at a third, neutral place? Should we sit down at a table, enhancing a sense of structure to the interview dynamic, or should we lounge comfortably (or semi-comfortably) on couches? Would I place a box of tissues nearby, taking care of participants and honoring the potential emotionality that accompanies this work, or was I assuming a certain emotiveness that might ultimately not arrive? What of the unused tissues?

And so, the interviews began.

Fully Inside It
Throughout the weeks of interviews that followed, I listened, with much eagerness and curiosity, and felt an immediate, overwhelming sense of relief. My relief stemmed in part from the realization that these women would not stand up mid-interview and storm out of the room; but beyond that, relief reflected my understanding that there were others like me—women who lived generations following the Holocaust, remained acutely entwined with their traumatic past, and yearned to explore this further. Most compelling of all was that words existed for these women's narratives—even the most disorganized or defensive narratives—and that, through language, each woman summoned her history, confronted painful realities, and reached towards creating a unique version of "truth." Yet the greatest common denominator amongst us was apparent: it was our willingness to show up in the first place, bearing our Stars for all to see.

The truth of the matter was that shame accompanied our Stars; this I knew inherently but became increasingly attuned to as the interviews progressed. What began as an external, deliberate attempt to "mark" and shame the Jews evolved into an internalized shame, incorporated into my identity and those of the women before me. Alongside that shame was a strong sense of guilt—how guilty we felt that a degree of shame about our history, culture, or religion existed in the first place. It was a difficult history, but one that we had survived and were *supposed* to consistently feel proud of; otherwise, the message was, "we" (no less than the entire Jewish people) had "lost."

At the same time, we clung to our pride—a deeply-rooted though somehow more fragile feeling surrounding our Stars. Pride was held high and paraded around, in a sort of exhibition, yet the exhibit occurred behind protective glass. Throughout the interviews, I sought to know more about this pride, and came to appreciate the strength and resilience that developed alongside our traumatic history. I thought of my family's Star and longed to be near it, to touch it, and to join in the act of fastening it to its framed place on the wall.

As the interviews progressed, I tapped into sadness about the unspoken truths surrounding our Stars, anger about the need to keep pages of our family autobiographies blank, and fear of what might be uncovered if these pages were filled. Last of all, I experienced eagerness and hope, aware of the mourning process that was taking place before me and sensing the development of community through our coming together to speak.

Nevertheless, our commonalities unfolded alongside our differences. While certain interviews conjured up associations to my own experiences, others did not. I noticed myself grow protective of some women, wanting to bolster them up and soothe their insecurities; yet I felt more challenging with others, pressing them to complete a thought or urging them to tackle a visibly challenging conflict. I took note of these discrepancies, wondering about individual differences amongst the interviewees and my own level of comfort in confronting certain experiences over others. Undoubtedly, my reactions and interventions varied from woman to woman, unfolding somewhat within and somewhat outside my awareness.

I consciously anticipated playing a number of roles in these interviews: that of a confidant, a sounding board, a bystander, or even a demanding interviewer. Yet the most difficult position to embody was that of the aggressor; at times, I perceived myself in this light following the slightest questioning of an interviewee. For example, at one point during a participant's depiction of her grandfather's experience in Eastern Europe, I asked a clarifying question about the manner in which her grandfather learned that his parents had been killed. The interviewee became frustrated by my question, informing me that she knows this story only as her grandfather had previously told it, and that whatever information she omits is likely unknown information to her. However, she then corrected herself and stated that she may accidentally forget to highlight adjacent stories, and that it would be okay for me to follow up with questions. Despite her permission, I found myself limiting my speech throughout the remainder of the interview.

Similarly, my own frustration arose when I sensed that ambiguity was unwelcome in the interview and therefore prematurely foreclosed. For example, a number of the interviewees spoke in a firm, sure voice that indirectly expressed, "I am confident of what I'm saying and I do not want that contested." At least one of the interviews felt like a power struggle from the start; her superimposed, intellectualized language and lack of affect pointed to the discomfort with the subject matter and the importance of boundaries in the room. I felt distanced in these moments and unable to make a connection, proceeding with caution so as not to cause pain. Yet, in curtailing a conversation that could potentially incite anger or shame, I felt my own frustration escalate; I treaded lightly with questions as I grew increasingly quiet, became increasingly blank, and, ultimately, was left increasingly drained.

These were difficult moments to tolerate and comprehend. How could I feel frustrated with an interviewee who was clearly struggling to convey her experience and simultaneously maintain her sense of self? How could I have anything but positive regard for someone who had been through so much and was willing to partake in this journey in the first place? What did it mean if I desired to push further, despite a clear communication that someone did not want to proceed? Indeed, the interviews tapped into my earliest childhood insecurities and replayed my own intergenerational dynamic: I was either the daring, questioning, potentially displeasing granddaughter, or the fearful, passive, compliant granddaughter who was left in an illusory state, with unanswered questions, a profound void of meaning, and a yearning for more.

At the same time, attempts to satisfy my own needs often led to the mobilization of guilt. For example, during one of the interviews,

I was aware of my desire for the interviewee to become increasingly emotive, thereby enhancing the intimacy between us. I longed for this contact—which stemmed from my own wish for kinship and connectedness—sustaining me in my search for a community that appreciates intergenerational Holocaust dynamics. Yet, I felt guilty for experiencing this desire, and as I walked her to the door and inquired about friends who might also be interested in sharing their stories, I felt like a needy, pushy, selfish interviewer who was inconsiderate of the participant's feelings or her time. Following her departure, as I reflected on this feeling, I wondered about the balancing of needs that took place in these interviews. Moreover, I came to reflect on the delicate weighing of needs that persisted throughout generations of my family. I wondered: could there be enough space for us all? How does one individual come to seek her own personal truth, particularly within a system that is fearful of pain? Do one woman's present-day needs and desires undermine the experiences of those who struggled before her? Who is entitled to speak of trauma, and what of all those bearing witness along the way?

Coming Out of the Experience, Or Not

Following the conclusion of my study, I unexpectedly found myself in a state of depression. This starkly conflicted with the encouragement and congratulations I received from friends and family around me, who lovingly emphasized that the completion of a dissertation should be a time of joy, pride, and relaxation. Yet, to their disbelief and perhaps a bit to my own, I was left feeling entirely isolated and overcome with grief. While my past experiences had demonstrated that endings are generally accompanied by loss and mourning, the loss surrounding this work was far more intense than I could have anticipated. The process had been an all-consuming, life-altering experience of extremes: it was at once draining and nourishing, disheartening but inspiring, startling while at the same time deeply familiar. I was fully inside it, without recognizing the existence of an "outside." And suddenly, it all came to an end.

The relationships I built throughout the course of this work undoubtedly shaped the void that was left behind. I developed and strengthened countless connections as I progressed through the experience, both interpersonal (with the ten interviewees, with my family, with my mentor, etc.) and intrapersonal (with my deepest fears, wishes, and needs, with my voice as expressed through writing, with the act of narration itself). My relationship with my grandmother spanned both realms: while we remained intimately connected in real life (though generally not through direct communication about this work), she was also an internalized figment of my mind throughout this process. Prior to but particularly following her passing, I turned to the image of my grandmother time and again, allowing me to encounter her world, learn from her thoughts, feelings and behaviors, and bump up against her way of being. With the summation of my study, this active and vigorous link seemed, somehow, to grow more passive and dimmed. Holding onto my sorrow soon became a conflictual experience in and of itself; while on the one hand I felt that I could never adequately mourn the multifaceted losses surrounding this work, I also questioned whether I retained my grief as a way of maintaining a connection to her.

Further adding to that void was the shocking realization that having invested so much of myself into this work did not necessarily mean that the people in my life would read it. This ranged from certain family members to friends and even to my therapist, most of whom read the "personal parts" related to my individual experience but could not muster their time or energy for the interviewees' narratives. Members of my dissertation committee themselves admitted on the day of my dissertation defense that they read the first few narratives and then set the work aside. I felt shocked, hurt, and misunderstood, confused about the impact of the stories and of my interpretations. Was the work entirely too much? Too long? Too dense? Should I have imparted these narratives in a more digestible form? Was it the content of the interviews, the reactions it elicited, or the act of bearing witness that turned people away? While I recognized the committee members' resistance to personal history, suffering, and memory, my own intergenerational dynamics surfaced once more—perhaps this material should not have been touched, or maybe I did not have a right to circulate, let alone verbalize, these thoughts. I feared the interviewees' reactions as well, and experienced a great deal of guilt while contemplating publishing my work. Nevertheless, while I continued to struggle with the question of whether my own needs and desires were warranted, I came to recognize and understand this pattern within a multi-generational perspective.

As time and the immediacy of the experience passed, others' reactions grew faint and the personal significance of my work began to shift.

I reflected on "trauma," which originates from the Greek word "a wound," and came to regard the completed manuscript as my "trauma baby": its traumatic nature contained generations of knowledge and spoke of truths that were difficult to bear. I had given birth to something entirely unique to me, containing those parts of myself that I would hope to transmit to future generations, those parts that I had long kept hidden, as well as those parts that I did not know to exist. And, with its birth, it bestowed an incredible gift—it held up a mirror before me, pointing to invaluable insights about my reality and about my sense of self, as a granddaughter, as a psychologist, and, a few years later, as a mother in this world.

Looking back, while I had attempted to prepare myself for the experience that I thought lay before me, there was no way to anticipate the journey ahead. I had told myself, "By initiating this quest, I will have to confront generations of silence and my own ambivalence surrounding my search for truth." But how could I have known what this really meant? How could I have envisioned so fully enveloping myself in this work, living and breathing a world of trauma? It is amusing to recall a time when I sought to maintain distance between myself and this experience; in the end, it was the impossibility of distance and the breakdown of silence that led "to a new sphere of freedom." And as my grandparents' belongings continue to be divvied up amongst family members, one item will travel across the world to me: that little yellow Star, waiting to be hung in my apartment, inviting questions that I hope will no longer go unasked. Who knows—one day, I may even remove the Star from its protective encasing of glass.

REFERENCES

3GNY: A NYC-Based Group for Grandchildren of Holocaust Survivors. (n.d.) Retrieved August 1, 2009, from http://www.3g-ny.org/.

Améry, J. (1998). *At the mind's limit: Contemplations by a survivor on Auschwitz and its realities*. (S. and S.P. Rosenfeld, Trans.) Bloomington: Indiana University Press.

Appelfeld, A. (1995, April 20). Fifty years after the Great War. *Yediot Aharonot*, p. 28.

Arad, G.N. (2003). Israel and the Shoah: A tale of multifarious taboos. *New German Critique, 90*, 5-26.

Atkinson, J. (2002). *Trauma trails—recreating song lines: The transgenerational effects of trauma in indigenous Australia*. North Melbourne: Spinifex Press.

Auerhahn, N.C., & Laub, D. (1998). Intergenerational memory of the Holocaust. In Y. Danieli (Ed.), *International Handbook of Multigenerational Legacies of Trauma* (p. 21-41). New York: Plenum Press.

Auerhahn, N.C., & Prelinger, E. (1983). Repetition in the concentration camp survivor and her child. *International Review of Psychoanalysis, 10*, 31-46.

Bachar, E., Cale, M., Eisenberg, J., & Dasberg, H. (1994). Aggression expression in grandchildren of Holocaust survivors: A comparative study. *Israeli Journal of Psychiatry and Related Disciplines, 31* (1), 41–47.

Balint, E. (1963). On being empty of oneself. *International Journal of Psychoanalysis, 44*, 470-480.

Bar-On, D. (1995) *Fear and hope: Three generations of the Holocaust*. Cambridge: Harvard University Press.

Bar-On, D. (2008). Forward. In H. Wiseman & J. P. Barber, *Echoes of the trauma: Relational themes and emotions in children of Holocaust survivors* (p. ix-xiii). New York: Cambridge University press.

Bar-Tal, D. (2001). Why does fear override hope in societies engulfed by intractable conflict, as it does in the Israeli society? *Political Psychology, 22*(3), 601-627.

Berant, E., & Hever, H. (in press). The granddaughters of female Holocaust survivors on their maternal side. In M. Rieck (Ed.), *The Holocaust: Its traumatic and intergenerational effects in comparison to other persecution, and its reflection in the arts*. Berlin: Verlag Irene Regener.

Berger, A.L. (1990). Bearing witness: Second generation literature of the "Shoah." *Modern Judaism, 10*(1), 43-63.

Bergmann, M.S., & Jucovy, M.E. (Eds.). (1990). *Generations of the Holocaust*. New York: Columbia University Press, reprint. (Originally published by Basic Books, 1982).

Berman, E. (1985). *From war to war: Cumulative trauma*. Paper presented at a meeting of the Israel Association of Psychotherapists.

Bion, W.R. (1959). Attacks on linking. *International Journal of Psychoanalysis, 40*, 308-315.

Bollas, C. (1989). *The shadow of the object: Psychoanalysis of the unthought known.* New York: Columbia University Press.

Borowski, T. (1976). *This way for the gas, ladies and gentlemen* (B. Vedder, Trans.). England: Penguin Books.

Boulanger, G. (2005). From voyeur to witness: Recapturing symbolic function after massive psychic trauma. *Psychoanalytic Psychology, 22*, 21-31.

Caruth, C. (Ed.). (1995). *Trauma: Explorations in memory.* Baltimore: The Johns Hopkins University Press.

Celan, P. (1958). Speech on the Occasion of Receiving the Literature Prize of the Free Hanseatic City of Bremen, as quoted in *Selected Poems and Prose of Paul Celan* (J. Felstiner, Trans.). New York: W.W. Norton & Company, 2001, 395.

Chaitin, J. (2003). "Living with" the past: Coping and patterns in families of Holocaust survivors. *Family Process 42*(2), 305-322.

Charles, M. (2003). The intergenerational transmission of unresolved mourning: Personal, familial, and cultural factors. *Samiksa: Journal of the Indian Psychoanalytic Society, 54*, 65-80.

Cole, T. (2002). Representing the Holocaust in America: Mixed motives or abuse? *The Public Historian, 24* (4), 127-131.

Coleridge, S.T. (1798). "The Rime of the Ancient Mariner." In E. H. Coleridge (Ed.), *The complete poetical works of Samuel Taylor Coleridge* (p. 186-209). Retrieved from http://www.gutenberg.org/files/29090/29090-h/29090-h.htm

Coser, L.A. (1992). Introduction. In M. Halbwachs, *On collective memory* (p. 1-34). Chicago: The University of Chicago Press.

Cyrulnik, B. (2005). *The whispering of ghosts: Trauma and resilience* (S. Fairfield, Trans.). New York: Other Press (Original work published 2003).

Cyrulnik, B. (2007). *Talking of Love: How to overcome trauma and remake your life story.* (D. Macey, Trans.) New York: Penguin Books. (Original work published 2005).

Danieli, Y. (1981). Countertransference in the treatment and study of Nazi Holocaust survivors and their children. *Victimology, 5*, 45-53.

Danieli, Y. (1984). Psychotherapists' participation in the conspiracy of silence about the Holocaust. *Psychoanalytic Psychology, 1*, 23-42.

Danieli, Y. (1988). The heterogeneity of post-war adaptation in families of Holocaust survivors. In R.L. Braham (Ed.), *The Psychological perspectives of the Holocaust and of its aftermath* (p. 109-127). Holocaust Studies Series. Boulder, CO: Social Science Monographs.

Davoine, F., & Gaudillière, J.M. (2004). *History beyond trauma: Whereof one cannot speak, thereof one cannot stay silent.* New York: Other Press.

Derrida, J. (1994) *Specters of Marx: The state of the debt, the work of mourning, and the new international.* (P. Kamuf, Trans.) Great Britain: Routledge. (Original work published 1993).

Diamant, A. (1997). *The Red Tent*. New York: St. Martin's Press.
Doneson, J.E. (1996). Holocaust revisited: A catalyst for memory or trivialization? *The Annals of the American Academy of Political and Social Science, 548* (1), 70-77.

Eizenstat, S.E. (1990). Loving Israel—Warts and all. *Foreign Policy, 81*, 87-105.
Elbedour, S., Bastien, D.T., & Center, B.A. (1997). Identity formation in the shadow of conflict: Projective drawings by Palestinian and Israeli Arab children from the West Bank and Gaza. *Journal of Peace Research, 34*(2), 217-231.
Epstein, H. (1979). *Children of the Holocaust: Conversations with sons and daughters of survivors*. New York: G.P. Putnam's Sons.
Ewing, K.P. (2004). Anthony Molino in conversation with Katherine Ewing. In A. Molino (Ed.), *Culture, subject, psyche: Dialogues in psychoanalysis and anthropology* (p. 80-97). Connecticut: Wesleyan University Press.

Felman, S., & Laub, D. (1992). *Testimony: Crises of witnessing in literature, psychoanalysis, and history*. Great Britain: Routledge, Chapman and Hall, Inc.
Felsen, I. (1998).Transgenerational transmission of effects of the Holocaust: The North American research perspective. In Y. Danieli (Ed.), *International Handbook of Multigenerational Legacies of Trauma* (p. 43-68). New York: Plenum Press.
Fink, R. (1999). *A clinical introduction to Lacanian psychoanalysis: Theory and technique*. Cambridge: Harvard University Press.
Fonagy, P. (2001). *Attachment theory and psychoanalysis*. New York: Other Press.
Fossion, P., Rejas, M., Servais, L., Pelc, I., & Hirsch, S. (2003). Family approach with grandchildren of Holocaust survivors. *American Journal of Psychotherapy, 57*(4), 519-527.
Fraiberg, S., Adelson, E., & Shapiro, V. (1975). Ghosts in the nursery: A psychoanalytic approach to the problems of impaired infant-mother relationships. *Journal of the American Academy of Child Psychiatry, 14* (3), 387-421.
Frankl, V. (2006). *Man's search for meaning*. Boston, MA: Beacon Press.
Freud, S. (1924). The loss of reality in neurosis and psychosis. *The Standard Edition of the Complete Psychological Works of Sigmund Freud, Volume XIX* (1923-1925): *The Ego and the Id and Other Works*, 181-188.

Gampel, Y. (1992). I was a Shoah child. *British Journal of Psychotherapy, 8*(4), 391-400.
Garber, Z., & Zuckerman, B. (1989). Why do we call the Holocaust "The Holocaust?" An inquiry into the psychology of labels. *Modern Judaism 9*(2), 197-211.
Garon, J. (2004). Skeletons in the Closet. *International Forum of Psychoanalysis, 13*, 84-92.
Grotstein, J.S. (1990a). The "black hole" as the basic psychotic experience: Some newer psychoanalytic and neuroscience perspectives on psychosis. *Journal of American Academy of Psychoanalysis, 18*, 29-46.
Grotstein, J.S. (1990b). Nothingness, meaninglessness, chaos, and the "black hole" I—The importance of nothingness, meaninglessness and chaos in psychoanalysis. *Contemporary Psychoanalysis, 26* (2), 257-290.

Halbwachs, M. (1992). *On collective memory* (L. Coser, Trans.). Chicago: The University of Chicago Press (Original work published 1941).

Herman, J. (1992). *Trauma and recovery: The aftermath of violence—from domestic abuse to political terror.* New York: Basic Books.

Hutton, P. (1994). Sigmund Freud and Maurice Halbwachs: The problem of memory in historical psychology. *The History Teacher, 27*(2), 145-158.

Jacobson, D.C. (1988). "Kill your ordinary common sense and maybe you'll begin to understand": Aharon Appelfeld and the Holocaust. *AJS Review, 13*(1), 129-152.

Jacobson, D.C. (1994). The Holocaust and the Bible in Israeli poetry. *Modern Language Studies, 24*(4), 63-77.

Josselson, R., Lieblich, A., & McAdams, D. P. (Eds.). (2003). *Up close and personal: The teaching and learning of narrative research.* Washington, DC: American Psychological Association.

Kaplan, L.J. (1996). *No voice is ever wholly lost: An exploration of the everlasting attachment between parent and child.* New York: Simon & Schuster.

Kestenberg, J.S. (1972). Psychoanalytic contributions to the problem of children of survivors from Nazi persecution. *Israel Annals of Psychiatry and Related Disciplines, 10*, 249-265.

Kestenberg, J.S. (1989). Coping with losses and survival. In D.R. Dietrich and P.C. Shabad (Eds.), *The Problem of Loss and Mourning: Psychoanalytic Perspectives* (p. 381-403). Madison, WI: International University Press, 381-403.

Kestenberg, J.S., & Brenner, I. (1996). *Last witness: The child survivor of the Holocaust.* Washington, DC: American Psychiatric Press.

Klein, M. (1948). A contribution to the theory of anxiety and guilt. *International Journal of Psychoanalysis, 29*, 114-123.

Koenig, S. (1952). Israeli culture and society. *The American Journal of Sociology, 58*(2), 160-166.

Lacan, J. (1968). *The language of the self: The function of language in psychoanalysis.* (A. Wilden, Trans.). Baltimore, MD: Johns Hopkins University Press.

Langer, L.L. (1991). *Holocaust testimonies: The ruins of memory.* New Haven: Yale University Press.

Lanzmann, C. (Director and producer). (1985). *Shoah* [Motion picture]. France: Les Films Aleph, Historia Films, 566 min.

Laub, D., & Auerhahn, N.C. (1985). Prologue. *Psychoanalytic Inquiry, 5*, 1-8.

Levi, P. (1989). *The drowned and the saved.* (R. Rosenthal, Trans.). New York: Vintage International (Original work published 1986).

Litvak-Hirsch, T., & Bar-On, D. (2006). To rebuild lives: A longitudinal study of the influences of the Holocaust on relationships among three generations of women in one family. *Family Process, 45*(4), 465-483.

Matte Blanco, I. (1988). *Thinking, feeling, and being: Clinical reflections on the fundamental antinomy of human beings and world.* London: Routledge.

Midgley, N. (2006). Psychoanalysis and qualitative psychology: Complementary or contradictory paradigms? *Qualitative Research in Psychology, 3* (3), 213-232.

Miller, A. (1997). *The drama of the gifted child* (3rd ed.) (R. Ward, Trans.). New York: Basic Books (Original work published 1979).

Mintz, A. (2001). *Popular culture and the shaping of Holocaust memory in America.* Seattle: University of Washington Press.

Mork, G. (1980). Teaching the Hitler period: History and morality. *The History Teacher, 13*(4), 509-522.

Neusner, J. (1973). The implications of the Holocaust. *The Journal of Religion, 53*(3), 293-308.

Novick, P. (1999). *The Holocaust in American life.* New York: Houghton Mifflin Company.

Novick, P. (2003). The American national narrative of the Holocaust: There isn't any. *New German Critique, 90,* 27-35.

Ogden, T. (2001). *Conversations at the frontier of dreaming.* Northvale, NJ: Jason Aronson.

Ogden, T. (2004). The art of psychoanalysis: Dreaming undreamt dreams and interrupted cries. *International Journal of Psychoanalysis, 85,* 857-877.

O'Loughlin, M. (2006). On knowing and desiring children: The significance of the unthought known. In G. Boldt & P. Salvio (Eds.), *Love's return: Psychoanalytic essays on childhood teaching and learning.* New York: Routledge.

O'Loughlin, M. (2007). Bearing witness to troubled memory. *Psychoanalytic Review, 94*(2), 191-212.

O'Loughlin, M. (2008). Radical hope, or death by a thousand cuts? The future for indigenous Australians. *Arena Journal, 29/30,* 175-201.

Packer, M.J., & Addison, R.B. (1989). *Entering the circle: Hermeneutic investigation in psychology.* Albany, New York: State University of New York Press.

Pontalis, J-B. (2002). *En marge des jours* (In the margins of the days). Paris: Gallimard. [Translated by and cited in Garon, 2004.]

Rebhun, U. (2004). Jewish identity in America: Structural analyses of attitudes and behaviors. *Review of Religious Research, 46* (1), 43-63.

Reilly, J. (1986, Winter). Maus: A survivor's tale [Review of the book *Maus: A survivor's tale,* A. Spiegelman]. *The Journal of Historical Review, 7*(4), 478. Available from Institute of Historical Review website: http://www.ihr.org/jhr/v07/v07p478_Reilly.html

Rogers, A.G. (2006). *The unsayable: The hidden language of trauma.* New York: Random House.

Rubenstein, I., Cutter, F., & Templer, D.I. (1989–1990). Multigenerational occurrence of survivor syndrome symptoms in families of Holocaust survivors. *Omega: Journal of Death and Dying, 20* (3), 239–244.

Sagi-Schwartz, A., van IJzendoorn, M.H., Grossmann, K., Joels, T., Grossmann, K., Scharf, M., Koren-Karie, N., & Alkalay, S. (2003). Attachment and traumatic stress in female Holocaust child survivors and their daughters. *American Journal of Psychiatry, 160* (6), 1086-1092.

Sagi-Schwartz, A., van IJzendoorn, M.H., & Bakermans-Kranenburg, M.J. (2008). Does intergenerational transmission of trauma skip a generation? No meta-analytic evidence for tertiary traumatization with third generation of Holocaust survivors. *Attachment & Human Development, 10*(2), 105-121.

Scharf, M. (2007). Long-term effects of trauma: Psychosocial functioning of the second and third generation of Holocaust survivors. *Development and Psychopathology, 19* (2), 603-622.

Segev, T. (1991). *The seventh million: The Israelis and the Holocaust.* New York: Owl Books.

Sigal, J.J. (1998). Long-term effects of the Holocaust: Empirical evidence for resilience in the first, second, and third generation. *Psychoanalytic Review, 85*(4), 579-585.

Sigal, J. J., DiNicola, V. F., & Buonvino, M. (1988). Grandchildren of survivors: Can negative effects of prolonged exposure to excessive stress be observed two generations later? *Canadian Journal of Psychiatry, 33* (3), 207-212.

Solomon, Z. (1993). *Combat Stress Reaction: The enduring toll of war.* New York: Plenum Press.

Solomon, Z. (1998). Transgenerational effects of the Holocaust: The Israeli research perspective. In Y. Danieli (Ed.), *International Handbook of Multigenerational Legacies of Trauma* (p. 69-83). New York: Plenum Press.

Spiegelman, A. (1986). *Maus I: A survivor's tale: My father bleeds history.* New York: Pantheon Books.

Spiegelman, A. (1991). *Maus II: A survivor's tale: And here my troubles began.* New York: Pantheon Books.

Sullivan, H.S. (1968). *The interpersonal theory of psychiatry.* New York: W,W. Norton.

Talby-Abarbanel, M. (2011). "Secretly attached, secretly separate" Art, dreams, and transference-countertransference in the analysis of a third generation Holocaust survivor. In A.B. Druck, C. Ellman, N. Freedman, & A. Thaler, (Eds.) *A new Freudian synthesis: Clinical process in the next generation* (p. 219-237). London: Karnac Books Ltd.

Tarantelli, C.B. (2003). Life within death: Towards a metapsychology of catastrophic psychic trauma. *International Journal of Psychoanalysis, 84,* 915-928.

Taub, M. (1997). The challenge to popular myth and conventions in recent Israeli drama. *Modern Judaism, 17*(2), 133-162.

Weiss, M. (1997). Bereavement, commemoration, and collective identity in contemporary Israeli society. *Anthropological Quarterly, 70*(2), 91-101.
Wiesel, E. (1961). *Night*. New York: Hill & Wang.
Wiseman, H., & Barber, J. P. (2008). *Echoes of the trauma: Relational themes and emotions in children of Holocaust survivors.* New York: Cambridge University Press.

INDEX

3GNY, 180-181
Abuse, 14, 23, 31, 98-99, 106-107, 109-111
Addison, R.B., 49
Adelson, E., 25
Agency, 22, 34, 38
A-letheia, 29
Aliyah, 16, 56
Améry, J., 20
Anesthetizing of feelings, 90, 94
Anger, 61, 81-82, 87, 99-101, 109-111, 113, 135, 154-155, 157-158, 165, 186
Anti-Semitism, 118, 125, 149-150
Anxiety, 24, 36, 39, 85, 111-112, 123, 133, 138, 158-159. *See also* Panic
Appelfeld, A., 34
Arad, G.N., 33-36
Atkinson, J., 41
Auerhahn, N.C., 28-29

Bachar, E., 41
Bakermans-Kranenburg, M.J., 41
Barber, J.P., 43
Bar-On, D., 34, 41-43, 45-46, 56
Bar-Tal, D., 36, 37
Bastien, D.T., 38
Bear witness, 14, 19, 28, 56, 105
Berant, E., 43-44
Berman, E., 39
Bion, W.R., 24
Black and white thinking, 82, 89
Bollas, C., 52, 160
Borowski, T., 20
Boulanger, G., 24
Boundaries, Implementation of, 13, 95, 134-137
   Violation of, 107-108

Cale, M., 41

"Camp," the word, 12, 54-55
Celan, P., 20, 25
Center, B.A., 38
Chaitin, J., 44
Charles, M., 28-29
Cole, T., 31
Coleridge, S.T., 7
Collective memory, 30, 51
   Israelis and the Holocaust, 33-40
   Jewish Americans and the Holocaust, 30-33. *See also* National narrative
Combat, 37-39
Combat Stress Reaction, 39
Community, 35, 37, 39, 96, 140, 180-181, 186, 188
Compartmentalization, 29, 121-122
Concentration camp, 26, 43, 54-57, 62, 82, 102, 104, 120, 156, 162, 169
   Auschwitz, 13, 14, 16, 17, 32, 60, 64, 79, 83, 102, 103
   See also "Camp," the word
Constructivist, 31
Coping style, 44
Coser, L.A., 30, 39
Countertransference, 11, 49, 93
"Cut out unconscious," 21
Cutter, F., 40
Cyrulnik, B., 65, 68, 78, 105, 176-180

Danieli, Y., 44, 93, 95
Dasberg, H., 41
Davoine, F., 20-21, 24-25, 29-30, 36-37, 66, 80, 90, 94
Denial, 15, 28, 34, 42, 66, 90, 155, 161, 180
Depression, 106-107, 134, 137-139, 165, 188
Derrida, J., 69-70
Diamant, A., 140

— 198 —

Index

Disarticulation, 22-23.
Dissociation, 13, 14, 15, 24, 155, 156, 161, 178, 180
Dolls, 97-98
Doneson, J.E., 31-32
Dreams, 13, 45, 73, 79, 149, 151, 158-159, 173-174. *See also* Nightmares

Eating disorder, 171-172, 174
   Anorexia, 13, 171
   Binging, 13, 132, 137
   Purging, 13, 137. *See also* Food; Starvation
Eichmann trial, 35
Eisenberg, J., 41
Elbedour, S., 38
Emotional. *See* "Overly" emotional
Empathy/sympathy, 80-81, 139
   Parent's empathic attunement, 28
Enactment, 13, 14, 25-29, 45, 58-59, 91, 104, 110, 129-130, 157, 162, 165. *See also* Repetition
Enmeshment, 86, 135, 137
Envy, 73, 81, 147
Ewing, K.P., 48
Exceptionalist, 31

Fascination with mass destruction, 90
Fear, 11, 12, 34, 36-37, 47, 62, 68, 85-86, 90, 103, 109-112, 114-116, 119, 122-126, 132-133 137-138, 149-150, 153, 170, 172, 185, 186, 189
Felman, S., 32-33, 56
Felsen, I., 40
Fictionalization, 22
Fink, B., 24
Food, 14, 26, 59-60, 67, 97, 98-99, 100, 102-104, 110, 115, 137, 164
Feeding a baby, 113-115, 147
Forced to eat, 60, 98-99, 102-104

Hoarding of, 103
   See also Eating disorders; Starvation
Fossion, P., 44
Fraiberg, S., 25

Gampel, Y., 96-97
Garon, J., 77, 80
Gaudillière, J.-M., 20-21, 24-25, 29-30, 36-37, 66, 80, 90, 94
Ghost, 13, 25, 27, 65, 68-70, 78, 124, 130
Goodbyes, meaning of, 16, 17, 174
"Good enough," 13, 151-152, 165, 167
Grandchildren. *See* Third generation
Gratitude, 114-116
Grief, 45, 105, 144, 148, 188-189
Grotstein, J.S., 23
Group identity. *See* Collective memory
Guilt, 13, 27, 34, 57-59, 64, 65, 73, 74, 82, 85, 90, 92, 93, 120, 151-152, 165, 171-173, 186, 187-188, 189

Halbwachs, M., 30
Hate, 90, 125-126, 150, 152-153
Herman, J., 66
Hever, H., 43-44
Hierarchy of suffering, 56-57, 80-81
Hirsch, S., 44

Idealization, 13, 39, 71-72, 86-88
Identification with the aggressor, 90
Individuation. *See* Separation/individuation
Intellectualization, 170, 187
Intergenerational transmission of trauma. *See* Transmission of trauma
Interpretative research, 11
Interviews of present research, 11-12, 15, 18, 45, 47-49, 61-62,

176-177, 179, 181, 184-188
Psychoanalytic interviews, 11, 48, 176
Interviewees. *See* Participants of present research
Introjection, 126, 165
Israel Defense Forces (IDF), 43
Israeli identity, 33-40, 141-142, 145-147

Jewish
   Carry on being, 14, 120
   Dating/marrying a non-Jew, 53, 59, 122-123, 128-130, 131
   Identity, 33, 40, 118, 120, 123-124, 130-131, 145-147
Josselson, R., 49

Kaplan, L.J., 25-28, 51-52, 56, 58, 72, 149, 181
Kestenberg, J.S., 25, 58
Kindertransport, 16
Koenig, S., 35

Lacan, J., 24
Langer, L.L., 20, 22, 32, 34-35, 36, 38
Language, 17, 19, 20, 21, 23-24, 47, 49, 54-55, 67, 78, 97, 105, 119, 125, 136, 143, 181, 185. *See also* Unsayable
Lanzmann, C., 20, 32-33
Laub, D., 20, 28-29, 32-33, 56, 152
Levi, P., 7, 20
Lieblich, A., 49
Litvak-Hirsch, T., 42
Log, interviewer's, 49
Loss, 36, 42, 45, 47, 68-70, 78, 92, 115, 130, 141, 147, 149, 152, 181, 188-189

Massada, 30
Mastery, 61, 64, 130, 132-133, 139
Matte Blanco, I., 23
McAdams, D.P., 49

Memorialization of the dead, 27, 72
Memory receptacle, 52, 132-133.
Mental health profession, 126, 138
Mental illness, 102-103
Miller, A., 183
Mintz, A., 31
Motherhood, 43, 75, 108-109, 112-114, 141, 147, 164, 190
Mourning, 25-26, 28, 39, 42, 52, 55, 63, 181, 186, 189

Names, 60-61, 65, 68, 77, 78-79, 105, 125, 145-147, 174-175
Narratives. *See* Interviews of present research
National narrative, 30-31, 33, 39. *See also* Collective memory
Nazi, being called a, 14, 90, 93
Nazi Germany/ Nazi Europe/ Nazi times, 13, 16, 85, 92, 97, 126
Neusner, J., 33
"Never forget," 18, 51, 123-124, 136
Nightmares, 13, 14, 32, 53, 73, 79-80, 159-160. *See also* Dreams
Novick, P., 30-31

Obesity, 26, 133. *See also* Eating disorder; Food
Obsessive-compulsive, 13, 64-65, 74, 176
Ogden, T., 23, 24
"Overly" emotional, 15, 17, 156, 162-163, 167-169
Overprotective, 84-86, 133
Ownership, 29, 74, 80-81, 119-120

Packer, M.J., 49
Panic, 14, 27, 85, 112-113, 138
Paranoia, 47, 149
Participants of present research, 18, 47-49, 176-178, 179, 184-188, 189
Pelc, I., 44
Perversion of judgment, 90

Pride, 14, 16, 37, 38, 73, 81, 119-121, 124, 127, 186
"Primary meaninglessness," 23
Projection, 82, 126, 165
Projective identification, 25
Psychoanalytic interviews. *See* Interviews of present research
Psychotic/ Insane, 14, 21, 24, 92-94, 95
PTSD (Posttraumatic Stress Disorder), 39, 132-133

Rational and irrational, 92-93
Rebelliousness, 13, 14, 128-129, 131
Reenactment. *See* Enactment
Reilly, J., 22
Rejas, M., 44
Repetition, 58, 69, 99, 129, 131, 162. *See also* Enactment
Repression, 21, 34, 150, 181
Resilience, 18, 30, 40, 176-181, 186
Revenant. *See* Ghost
Revival of the catastrophes, 90
Rogers, A.G., 23-24, 77, 103-104
Rubenstein, I., 40

Sabras, 34, 36, 146
Sadness, 14, 32, 132, 137-138, 143-144, 156, 166, 186
Sagi-Schwartz, A., 41, 179
Scharf, M., 43
Secret, 27-28, 52-53, 65-66, 68, 77, 107-108, 119, 131, 144, 149. *See also* Silence
Segev, T., 35, 37, 40
Self-esteem, 36, 127
Separation/individuation, 43, 86, 137-138
Servais, L., 44
Shame, 14, 42, 73, 106-107, 110, 117-121, 183, 185-186
Shapiro, V., 25
Shoah
Definition of, 20

Film by Claude Lanzmann, 20, 32, 184
Shtetl, 145-146
Sigal, J.J., 40
Silence, 12, 17, 18, 27-28, 31, 33-34, 42-43, 44, 51-54, 66-67, 77, 93, 95, 108, 110, 118-119, 143, 148-149, 163, 181, 184, 190. *See also* Language; Secret
Six-Day War, 35, 36
Solomon, Z., 36, 38, 39
Somatization, 104-105
Spiegelman, A., 20, 22, 27
Splitting, 72-73, 87-88, 123, 141-142, 146
Star of David, 183
Starvation, 26, 99, 102-103, 115, 133. *See also* Eating disorder; Food
Suicide/ suicidal, 14, 103, 104, 105, 110, 115
Survivor guilt. *See* Guilt
Swastika, 14, 117-118
Symbolization. *See* Language
Symptom, 24, 44, 65, 66, 67, 105.

Talby-Abarbanel, M., 45
Tarantelli, C.B., 22-23, 24
Templer, D.I., 40
Testimonial momentum, 12
Thematic analysis, 49
Therapy, 14, 35, 45, 86, 108, 111-112, 122, 134, 155-156, 158, 160-164, 168
Third generation, 11, 13, 17, 40-46, 47, 49, 52, 65, 115, 126, 150, 165, 167, 176, 179-181
Tisha B'Av, 55
Transference, 29, 49
Transmission of trauma, 13, 15, 17-18, 24-26, 30, 37, 40-44, 51-52, 54, 57-60, 62, 64, 75, 91, 97, 107-108, 133, 144, 149, 153, 165, 170, 177, 179

Transposition, 25, 26, 58
Trauma trails, 41, 176, 179, 182
Trivialization, 32, 90

"Unsayable," 23-24, 77, 78, 103, 105.
    See also Language
Unthought known, 15, 52, 53, 160

van IJzendoorn, M.H., 41

Weiss, M., 37, 39
Wiesel, E., 20
Wiseman, H., 43
Witness, no such thing as, 20, 56, 57,
    152. *See also* Bear witness
Women as carriers of history, 15,
    140-141
Working through, 26, 39, 54, 58, 63,
    110, 163, 177

Yom Kippur War, 31, 35, 36

Zionism, 34, 35, 145, 149, 151-153

www.ingramcontent.com/pod-product-compliance
Ingram Content Group UK Ltd.
Pitfield, Milton Keynes, MK11 3LW, UK
UKHW021848140426
5217IPUK00022B/1660